THE BATTLE OF BRITAIN
A VISUAL HISTORY

Published by IWM, Lambeth Road, London SE1 6HZ
iwm.org.uk

ISBN 978-1-912423-51-4

A catalogue record for this book is available
from the British Library.

Printed and bound by Printer Trento
Colour reproduction by DL Imaging
Index by Nicola King

Front cover: HU 54420 (artificially coloured)
Back cover: HU 54418 (see page 71)

THE BATTLE OF BRITAIN

A VISUAL HISTORY

Anthony Richards

CONTENTS

INTRODUCTION

The Battle of Britain was a battle <u>for</u> Britain. We were young fighter pilots, scarcely schoolboys, but the cockpits of our fighter aeroplanes were all that stood between invasion of this country by the Germans. We'd seen what they'd done to the nationals abroad. We lived in this country and some of us lived within sight of our airfields. I used to fly often to Portsmouth and look down on my home, where my family was, in Chichester. Tangmere was being bombed ten miles away. It was all a very personal thing. When you got into your aeroplane, you felt the fears that everybody fears when going off to fight, but overpowering all that was this feeling that if you and all your chaps didn't do your damnedest on every operation then all these Germans were going to be flooding over your country, your homes, and destroying everything that was worth preserving. That was what it was all about.

This tribute to the air crew of the Battle of Britain, printed in 1940, reproduces the famous Churchill quote about 'The Few'.

(Pages 6–7) Runway Perspective by Eric Ravilious, 1942

This is how many remembered the Battle of Britain: as an intensely personal conflict, a firm stand by a small island nation against a larger, implacable foe who was determined to crush their resolve to stand up for freedom. For the people of Britain in 1940, to lose the fight would lead to the inevitability of invasion and occupation by Nazi Germany. But, as with so many other historical events, not only during the Second World War but throughout wider history, this basic narrative can be expanded to reveal a somewhat more complicated story.

We should recognise that any study of the Battle of Britain is faced with a number of difficulties right from the outset. For one thing, historians don't agree on what date the battle began. There was also no clear geographical boundary to the battle, no one event to indicate when it ended, and no clear overwhelming defeat of one protagonist by the other to indicate who actually won.

Further ambiguities arise from the overall public perception of the battle. Though people commonly remember it as an encounter between the British Royal Air Force (RAF)'s Fighter Command and the German Luftwaffe in the skies over southern Britain, there were many other elements to the nation's fight for survival. Additional offensive operations against Britain were taking place at the same time, with the German Navy busy blockading the country from receiving vital imports, while other parts of the RAF were employed against the serious ongoing threat of a German invasion. The aerial bombing of British cities in particular is often seen as a campaign in its own right, yet it also remains intrinsically linked to the course of the Battle of Britain.

To add yet another element of complexity, we should remember that the Battle of Britain could never really be considered as an outright British victory. It was, more accurately, an avoidance of defeat. This is not to downplay the importance of the battle and the necessity to fight – far

Neville Chamberlain (1869–1940), prime minister of the United Kingdom at the beginning of the Second World War. His perceived failure over the Norway campaign led to calls for his resignation, and this crisis was directly responsible for Churchill assuming the position of PM.

'Flash', a German Shepherd dog and mascot of No. 19 Squadron RAF, pictured seated on the nose of a Spitfire at Fowlmere, Cambridgeshire, in September 1940.

from it – but we should keep in mind that at the conclusion of 1940 neither side had any particular advantage to speak of. By the end of the year Britain had avoided a potential German invasion, yet was still isolated and facing a powerful foe. The battle had stopped Hitler from claiming a quick and 'cheap' victory, yet there would be further years of sacrifice ahead before the conflict could be truly won and brought to an end.

However, it is clear that the battle remains one of the vital moments of the war, if only to signify the first occasion when the aggression of Nazi Germany was legitimately thwarted. It was a defining turning point, not only in the history of the Second World War but in cultural and national terms as well. In the minds of many of us, the very name of the battle links it to 'home' and evokes the loyal defence of a nation by its population. The pilots of Fighter Command who flew into battle and risked their lives on a daily basis are still, to this day, granted a particularly special form of recognition. Even the machines they flew – the Spitfire and Hurricane fighters – are regarded in a unique light and continue to be at the heart of air shows and pageants to mark significant national occasions. The serious threat from aerial bombing confronted by civilians on a daily basis gave life to the so-called 'Blitz spirit', which similarly endures as a characteristic of national pride.

This sense of determination in the face of peril was perfectly illustrated by the promises made by Prime Minister Winston Churchill in his speech to the House of Commons on 4 June 1940. Despite the Nazi occupation of France and the hasty evacuation of British troops from Dunkirk and other Channel ports, the fight would go on.

> We shall prove ourselves once again able to defend our Island home, to ride out the storm of war, and to outlive the menace of tyranny, if necessary for years, if necessary alone. At any rate, that is what we are going to try to do. That is the resolve of His Majesty's Government – every man of them. That is the will of Parliament and the nation. The British Empire and the French Republic, linked together in their cause and in their need, will defend to the death their native soil, aiding each other like good comrades to the utmost of their strength... We shall go on to the end, we shall fight in France, we shall fight on the seas and oceans, we shall fight with growing confidence and growing strength in the air, we shall defend our Island, whatever the cost may be. We shall fight on the beaches, we shall fight on the landing grounds, we shall fight in the fields and in the streets, we shall fight in the hills; we shall never surrender...

But Britain would never carry on the fight 'alone' – it would receive vital and considerable support from Canada, South Africa, Australia, New Zealand, India and its wider colonial empire, in addition to forces from France, Poland, Czechoslovakia and elsewhere who had fled to Britain to carry on their own national fights in support of the wider

Allied cause. We cannot overstate the contribution of these individuals and nations. Some 2,937 British and overseas pilots fought on the Allied side throughout the Battle of Britain, with 544 losing their lives as a result. Even greater sacrifices were made by British civilians: during the period from July to December 1940 some 27,450 were killed and 32,000 more wounded, largely due to the bombing of British cities. While the Battle of Britain is commonly seen as a victory achieved by 'The Few', in a view championing the typically British appeal of an underdog fighting back against a larger aggressor, in reality the achievements of Fighter Command were heavily dependent on much wider support and an international level of commitment.

But even as we question the accuracy of some of the myths which have influenced the traditional narrative over many decades, the importance of the Battle of Britain remains, for it was a crucial fight against potential invasion. If the battle had been lost, the consequences would likely have been disastrous for the rest of the world. The means by which Germany's intentions were thwarted is the story of a nation's decision to stand against aggression, and in so doing, inspire both itself and its allies to fight back.

Squadron Leader Douglas Bader, commanding No. 242 (Canadian) Squadron RAF, with Squadron Leader Alexander 'Sasha' Hess, commander of No. 310 (Czech) Squadron RAF, at Duxford, Cambridgeshire, in September 1940.

(Pages 14–15) Winston Churchill (1874–1965), prime minister of the United Kingdom during the Battle of Britain and the leader forever associated with it.

Chapter One
BACKGROUND

The outcome and legacy of the First World War were instrumental in determining the next global conflict. Political instability and economic insecurity throughout the world during the 1920s and 1930s gave rise to extremism within many European nations. People looked to authoritarian leadership as an answer to their problems, with the fascist leader Benito Mussolini coming to power in Italy in 1922, and Adolf Hitler assuming the role of Germany's chancellor in 1933. Political opposition to both regimes was violently repressed, as aggressive nationalism became increasingly prominent throughout Europe.

By July 1936, much attention was centred on Spain, where right-wing nationalists led by General Franco and most of the country's armed forces sought to overthrow the left-wing republican government. Civil war erupted and would drag on for close to three years. While Britain preferred not to intervene on either side, perhaps remembering the way in which political and military promises had kick-started the global war in 1914, both Italy and Germany chose to support Franco and contributed to the nationalists achieving a victory by April 1939.

Many commentators regarded the Spanish Civil War as a potential 'dry run' for a larger European conflict, in particular because it revealed the advances which had been made in aerial warfare since the days of the First World War. It also served to generate a formidable reputation for Germany's highly trained Luftwaffe. Spain suffered significant bombing from the air, most infamously on the town of Guernica in the country's northern Basque region. Many hundreds of civilians were killed by bombs dropped by Italian and German aircraft, and the subsequent controversy over the justification for such military actions led to many worried predictions about how a future, larger European war might evolve.

Air power was one of the newest technologies adapted for conflict, and advances in aircraft design and engine capabilities meant an ever-increasing operational range. The Spanish bombing campaign had shown that modern aircraft could take off from home territory and drop bombs on another country's civilian population with relative ease, and this was a very real concern. Memories of the terrible effects of poison gas, first introduced to the battlefields of Belgium in 1915, combined with these fears to create nightmares of deadly gas bombs being dropped on modern towns and cities. Popular culture both embraced and encouraged such worries. H G Wells's science fiction novel *The Shape of Things to Come* (first published in 1933 and adapted for film in 1936) was particularly prescient, describing a global conflict with cities smashed to bits by aerial bombing.

Britain took such concerns very seriously during the 1930s and spent millions of pounds on air power, concentrating its resources on developing more advanced fighter technology. The Royal Air Force also

(Right) In this propaganda poster from the Spanish Civil War, red hands clutching daggers grow out of Italy and Germany to stab Spain. The hands are marked with the fascist emblems of each nation, while Spain is marked with broken chains and the Phrygian cap, a republican revolutionary symbol.

(Pages 16–17) Thousands of British troops line up on the beach at Dunkirk to await evacuation, during the final days of May 1940.

(Pages 20–21) German troops travel in rubber dinghies along a Norwegian fjord, as part of the German invasion of Norway in 1940.

ELDONITA DE COMISSARIAT DE PROPAGANDA DE LA GENERALITAT DE CATALUNYA.

created a new Bomber Command, largely intended as a deterrent to enemy bombing campaigns, and held stocks of mustard gas in readiness to use as retaliation. Civilian defence measures were also introduced across the country in order to reduce the expected high number of air raid casualties as far as possible. A particular fear was that air attacks would arrive with little or no warning, and so significant resources were spent on developing various forms of early-warning technology to anticipate incoming raids. Crucially, Britain's decision to concentrate on measures such as these to defend itself at home meant that there were much fewer resources, together with less inclination, to develop the nation's offensive capability. The main consequence of this strategy was that any major contribution to a military land campaign in Europe would effectively be out of the question by the end of the 1930s, as would be shown when Poland and other countries suffered occupation by Nazi Germany.

British fears of an imminent bombing attack by the Luftwaffe were therefore understandably high at the outbreak of war against Germany on 3 September 1939. On that date, it was found that 70 per cent of Londoners carried their gas masks with them at all times, in expectation of a sudden attack. But the subsequent period of 'Phoney War', in which a stalemate was largely maintained despite the French mobilising their forces and Britain sending a small Expeditionary Force to the Continent in support, led to a significant decline in expectations of an attack on Britain; by the end of March 1940 and in the face of an absent enemy, only one per cent of Londoners now carried gas masks. The British public were in fact completely justified in no longer expecting immediate air raids. Germany's war strategy in the air was instead based on combined operations with its army, utilising fast and hard-hitting attacks by both air and ground armour which would come to be known as Blitzkrieg or 'lightning war'. Long-range attacks on towns and cities, whether to target industrial infrastructure or inflict damage on civilian morale, were not yet part of the Nazis' plan.

But the situation would soon change, as the Phoney War developed into a very real conflict. On 9 April, German forces began to occupy Denmark and the same day mounted an airborne invasion of Norway. A small-scale British Expeditionary Force (BEF) was sent to Norway to fight alongside French and Polish troops, but they could do little to hold back the German occupation, which was consolidated by June. The so-called 'Norway Debacle' would threaten to bring down the British government, leading to intense parliamentary debate which would become, in effect, a vote of no confidence in Prime Minister Neville Chamberlain's continued leadership. Chamberlain suggested Winston Churchill as a suitable successor, due to the support that Churchill enjoyed from both sides of the house, and the new prime minister assumed office on 10 May. Yet Churchill was far from as popular as he might have wished, as test pilot Jeffrey Quill recalled many years later when asked about the handover of leadership in Britain.

Spanish refugees fleeing from the embattled city of Madrid in 1937, after the intense aerial bombing it suffered at the hands of the fascists.

(Left) The interior of Barcelona Cathedral, photographed after it was bombed by German and Italian aircraft at dawn on 19 June 1938, during the Spanish Civil War.

The German Army continued to use horses as one of their main forms of transportation throughout the war, as shown in this image from the Norwegian campaign of German horse-drawn artillery near Oslo on 14 April 1940.

The Allies sought to bolster the Norwegian resistance through their own expeditionary forces. Here, British troops are photographed talking to French and Polish (Independent Podhalan Rifles Brigade) soldiers, around a French Hotchkiss H39 tank in Steinsland, Norway, in 1940.

(Pages 28–29) Three of the armada of 'little ships' which brought the men of the British Expeditionary Force from the shores in and around Dunkirk to the safety of British warships and other vessels. 1 June 1940.

On the day that Churchill came to power, I called on an elderly couple who had been great friends of my parents. We were discussing the leadership question and I said, 'I wouldn't be surprised if old Churchill doesn't get into power.' The man, who was obviously a much older generation, said, 'Good heavens, I hope not!' It made me understand how greatly his generation of Englishmen distrusted Churchill. In their eyes, he was a rather wild man, politically.

It would take Churchill some time to convince the population that he was the right man for the job, and in the meantime the new PM faced a new immediate challenge. On the very same day that he took office, 10 May 1940, the German invasion of France and the Low Countries began. Just as the Expeditionary Force sent to Norway was of limited assistance, so the small-scale BEF sent to France proved to be of little help in stopping the German advance, and both French and British forces soon had to retreat, to be evacuated from the Channel ports. Samuel Love was a private with the 12th Field Ambulance RAMC and recalled the constant attention that the BEF received from the enemy during their flight to the French coast.

All the way up to Poperinghe, we were attacked by Dorniers and Messerschmitts. At Poperinghe, they slunk off and then you could see Jerry's tanks three or four hundred yards away coming round the bend of the hill. They started firing over open sights. After that, all these bombers came and dropped their shit on us. God, what a bloody mess. The population of Poperinghe was only five or six hundred and I don't think there were two bricks left standing, one on top of the other. We got out of there and three of us set off for Dunkirk on foot. The other nine were left behind and what happened to them nobody knows. It was about 90 miles to Dunkirk and you daren't bloody sleep. You had to keep going.

The involvement of the RAF in the Battle for France was low-key. Poor communication between the Allies together with France's insistence on short-range operations in support of the army (for which British pilots were ill-trained) reduced the impact of British air power. Hurricane fighters were sent in piecemeal but suffered huge losses: throughout May and June, 477 fighters were destroyed and 284 pilots killed. The new Spitfire fighter aircraft was also introduced into combat during the final evacuations from the coast, yet 155 were swiftly destroyed (65 alone in accidents, as pilots were still getting to grips with the complicated technology). The initial effectiveness of the Spitfire was far from all that had been hoped, yet one German pilot, Wolfgang Falck, recalled how the new British aircraft enjoyed some success in spoiling his own involvement in the Blitzkrieg attacks.

Winston Churchill addresses staff at the British
Embassy in Washington DC in May 1943. Standing
next to him is Lord Halifax, the foreign secretary,
who at one point seemed by far to be the most
likely candidate to replace Neville Chamberlain as
prime minister. Yet Halifax had no appetite to lead
Britain in war.

I was almost a victim during a dogfight with many Spitfires. My Messerschmitt 110 was too big, not manoeuvrable or fast enough. The Spitfires hit my tail and damaged my rudder. My aircraft was shaking like it was an old tram. I held the stick with both hands and took the aircraft down to the sea. That way I lost the Spitfire, and I flew over France and the British troops below. I didn't trust the aircraft, so then I tried to get up to 300 metres in case I had to use my parachute. As I climbed up again, three or four Spitfires got behind me, so I flew down again. I was flying so slowly that I lost them. The country was flat, but I was flying so low that I had to jump over the dykes that were two or three metres high. As I flew over one dyke, I saw an English soldier riding a bicycle just in front of me. He fell off the bicycle and I'm sure that he's told the story, 'A pig of a German pilot tried to knock me off my bicycle!' But if he'd thrown a stone at me, I could have been his victim.

It was only during the evacuations from Dunkirk that the RAF could contribute greater numbers of fighters, with Hurricanes and Spitfires now flying from bases in southern England to the limit of their range. By the end of 4 June, almost 340,000 troops had been rescued from the Continent over a period of nine days. The operations at Dunkirk and the other Channel ports would effectively mark the beginning of a period of almost continuous air combat for the defence of Britain. This was, finally, the kind of war that Britain had been expecting and had made preparations for. In a speech delivered to the House of Commons on 18 June, Churchill famously declared that, '[T]he Battle of France is over. I expect the Battle of Britain is about to begin.'

*

At the beginning of June 1940, many people in Britain expected a German invasion. The shock caused by the quick defeat of France and the hurried evacuation of troops and civilians from Dunkirk and elsewhere led to a great deal of confusion and uncertainty back home. Such feelings affected the British leadership, and the government was far from united on the question of what to do next. While most preferred to support Churchill's insistence on fighting on, some argued in favour of returning to the policy of appeasement with Hitler. The foreign secretary, Lord Halifax, was a particular supporter of negotiation, disliking Churchill's belligerent attitude and proposing instead a policy of 'common sense, not bravado'. But the public mood was largely with Churchill and a tense government meeting on 28 May had left Halifax isolated. Appeasement was increasingly seen as a policy which would consistently fail to work with such an untrustworthy opponent as Hitler, and supporters of diplomacy with Germany were from now on either marginalised or ignored – to many minds, continued belligerency was the only honourable option. Despite British society remaining split by geographical and class differences, the common attitude across the country was that a German invasion was

In this photograph taken in 1941 in the Suffolk village of Orford, members of the local invasion committee discuss some of the issues facing them should an invasion occur. The group includes a police constable, county councillor, member of Parliament, parish council chairman, district nurse and schoolmaster (who was also the senior Air Raid Precaution, or ARP, warden).

Lord Halifax photographed in Scarborough, North Yorkshire, in August 1940. He is shown inspecting a fortified strongpoint on the promenade at the seaside town.

likely to happen but that Britain should do everything in its power to prevent and obstruct it.

The British government began to implement new legislation and other measures to prepare the country for a potential invasion, and reinforced or enlarged existing organisations, such as the Air Raid Precautions services. The Air Raid Warden Service had been established as early as 1937, while the government had begun to distribute Anderson shelters (corrugated steel huts designed to be buried in gardens) in early 1939. Blackout regulations (the prevention of lights which might be used as navigational aids for night bombers) had been introduced on 1 September 1939. Amid these endeavours to prepare the civilian population for war, Churchill's government made a concerted effort to encourage those on the home front to remain cheerful and brave, epitomised by the propaganda message 'Keep Calm and Carry On'.

Particular efforts were made to prepare and fortify towns and villages located in the south-east of England, especially near the coast, where any invaders would arrive first. Hilda Cripps was involved in such preparations in her village of Great Wakering, located in Essex.

> The chairman of the parish council came and asked me to be on an invasion committee. I said I would, and the commander from Shoeburyness garrison came and told us that we must remain totally secret... He said, 'Your duty will be, as far as possible, to provide the essential things for living – food and drink. You won't be allowed on any roads; they will be entirely for my military. Do your best to prevent panic and keep some sort of semblance of life going.' And off he went.

> We expected saturation bombing before the invasion, so we took delivery of 420 papier-mâché coffins. They were stored in the loft of a building right in the middle of the high street. The next thing we did, we placed containers of rations at strategic points around the village that could be reached by field paths. We set aside one large house as a possible hospital, and a smaller one as an isolation hospital. We made a consensus of all the livestock – sheep, cows, pigs, chickens – and then decided the order in which they would be killed for food. Pigs and sheep first, then cows, but not those that were in milk, of course, and the chickens that were not laying. We visited every house in the village to find out whether there was anyone who might be available for cleaning, caring for people or preparing food. We all had overall responsibility for the committee, but we each had our own particular job and mine was for the water supply for the village. The first thing I did was to go to an elderly retired builder, who was able to give me information about a great many wells in the village. I went to Southend Water Company and asked if they could send someone to inspect the wells and tell me if the water in them was fit for drinking, which they did without any

query... Then I found out which farmers had water carts and these carts were made available to be sterilised and used to allocate water from the wells.

We were very ordinary people but we worked hard over these weeks. We used to meet down at the Congregational church when it was vital that we knew what the next overall move was. A little yellow triangle appeared on the old village school, which told the military authorities that any information given out there would be correct, because they'd had problems with quislings giving false information. The last thing we were told by the authorities was that if invasion did come, six of the committee would likely be shot by the Germans, so that the village wouldn't get in the way of invading German troops!

Along with these serious preparations were more unorthodox methods of defence which arose from the overall feeling in the country that every civilian should do their bit to defend Britain against the enemy. Ronald Oates recalled one example of such grim, yet perhaps somewhat misguided, determination.

I went into my friend's house and on her mother's wall were some beautiful carved wooden bellows. I went to examine them. 'Don't touch them!' said the mother. 'Why not?' 'They're full of pepper,' she said. 'Why on earth have you got pepper in them?' 'When the Germans come, I'm not letting them get away with it easy. I'm going to blow pepper at them.'

Richard Holborow was serving as a non-commissioned officer with the Gloucestershire Regiment, on home defence duties at Hythe in Kent. Invasion fears were rife and the constant state of vigilance within Britain inevitably led to widespread gossip and the spread of misinformation.

At this time there were many rumours flying about. Almost daily there was a scare of some sort or another, some of the favourites being that 'last night a mate of mine up the road definitely saw several Germans offshore in a rowing boat' or 'I heard last night that a lot of dead Germans were washed up on the other side of town'. The latter rumour could possibly have had a foundation of truth in it, as after the war was over it was widely reported that many Germans were drowned while exercising for their invasion. All rumours however provided interesting subjects for conversation, although they tended to fuel one's anxiety as to just what to expect in the days to come.

While people took precautionary measures on the home front, the armed forces carried out reactionary activities. The Royal Navy's Fleet Air Arm and the RAF's Coastal Command continued to reconnoitre German-controlled ports and bomb enemy shipping, while from the middle of May, Bomber Command undertook missions against German oil and transport targets in occupied Europe. The cost was high for both of these branches of the air force, however, with the first daylight raids undertaken by Bomber Command leading to almost suicidal loss rates. The beginning of July saw Bomber Command directed to attack anti-invasion targets in the French Channel ports, as well as their regular aircraft production, oil and communications goals. They achieved some modest success, though they were assigned an inadequate number of aircraft and pilots for the task. Still, the emphasis would continue to be on the defence of Britain rather than any overt offensive campaign.

But what were Hitler's actual plans for Britain? In truth, Germany's victory over France had been so swift that the Nazis had given little thought to what should happen next. Hitler's personal view of Britain was best characterised as a mixture of envy and contempt. While he hated what he regarded as the nation's decadence, he openly respected its famous history and greatly envied its naval power and colonial empire. Many Germans believed that they shared in Britain's Anglo-Saxon heredity and therefore had a lot in common with the British people. These perceived similarities encouraged the view shared by Hitler and the majority of Germans that Britain had entered the war unwillingly and with the Fall of France no longer had any reason to remain in the conflict. Some kind of political or diplomatic settlement was therefore the most likely outcome, especially considering the debate which had been going on within the British government as to whether they should strike a deal with the Nazis. However, if diplomatic pressure did not provoke such an agreement, Hitler would need to remove the threat posed by Britain so that he could concentrate his full military strength on the Eastern Front, where his real desires lay. The east held the valuable territory necessary for the Third Reich to expand, while a war against the Soviet Union would also mean a war against communism – the ideology most hated by the Nazis.

While Germany made continued efforts to reach some kind of diplomatic settlement with Britain, Churchill's belligerent refusal to surrender made it appear increasingly likely that outright attack and occupation may be the only option. Some elements within the Nazi leadership therefore began to lobby for a more aggressive approach. The German Navy in particular continued to push Hitler for a more hostile air and naval blockade of the British Isles, which in turn might pave the way for an invasion. Further encouraged by Foreign Minister Joachim von Ribbentrop's ardent hatred of Britain, Hitler issued a directive on 7 July which authorised preparations for 'the war against England' to begin. A week later, the German armed forces were instructed to prepare for a full invasion to begin sometime after 15 August. These instructions were consolidated on 16 July with the formal issue of Führer Directive No. 16 to order what was now known as Operation Sea Lion, the German invasion of Britain. This would

(Right) Introduced at the very beginning of September 1939, shortly before the outbreak of war, the blackout was one of the key measures of Air Raid Precautions. The absence of lights was intended to thwart enemy bombers, yet it caused great confusion among the British population. Special guidance was issued, such as this cycling poster.

(Pages 38–39) A rather posed photograph of a soldier standing watch behind beach defences 'somewhere in Southern Command', 15 October 1940. The original notes by the photographer reveal that the image was 'taken by request of GOC-in-C Southern Command, to be used as Christmas cards'.

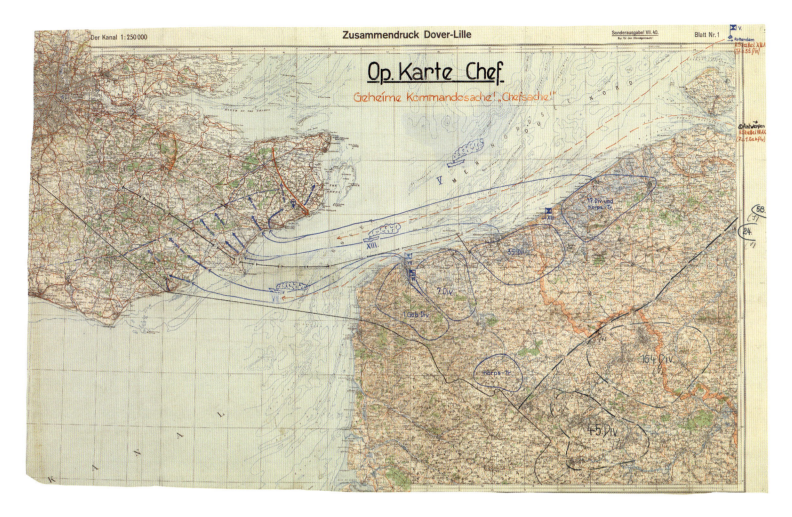

Op. Karte Chef

Geheime Kommandosache! „Chefsache!"

consist of a surprise landing on the south coast of England, between Ramsgate and the Isle of Wight. Crucially, the Germans recognised that such an operation would only prove successful if they could establish air superiority over southern England and secure a safe area of the Channel for the crossing. They appreciated that these conditions were far from straightforward to achieve, and that Germany had never undertaken such a major sea-based invasion before, and so they suspended the final decision until all diplomatic attempts to end the war with Britain had been exhausted. Their preferred option was still to force Britain into peace negotiations.

Hitler's patience was beginning to wear thin on 19 July as he gave a speech to the German parliament which included a 'last appeal to reason', expressing his argument that continuation of the war with Britain was solely down to the British people themselves and that such conflict could only bring disaster.

> A great world empire will be destroyed. A world empire which I never had the ambition to destroy or as much as harm. Alas, I am fully aware that the continuation of this war will end only in the complete shattering of one of the two warring parties. Mr Churchill may believe this to be Germany. I know it to be England. In this hour I feel

One of the planning maps prepared by the German 16th Army (AOK 16) for Operation Sea Lion, showing areas in France and the Low Countries for the concentration of the invasion forces, their routes across the Channel, and their lines of advance through southern England. Following landings between Dover and Dorset, the Germans intended to advance to capture London and the area south of a line from the Bristol Channel to the Wash.

(Left) Coastal Defences by Eric Ravilious, 1940. Between September and October 1940, official war artist Eric Ravilious was posted to Newhaven in East Sussex to paint coastal defences. The port was targeted as part of Operation Sea Lion and so was heavily fortified.

compelled, standing before my conscience, to direct yet another appeal to reason in England. I believe I can do this as I am not asking for something as the vanquished, but rather, as the victor, I am speaking in the name of reason. I see no compelling reason which could force the continuation of this war.

I regret the sacrifices it will demand. I would like to spare my Volk [people]. I know the hearts of millions of men and boys aglow at the thought of finally being allowed to wage battle against an enemy who has, without reasonable cause, declared war on us a second time.

But I also know of the women and mothers at home whose hearts, despite their willingness to sacrifice to the last, hang onto this last with all their might.

Mr. Churchill may well belittle my declaration again, crying that it was nothing other than a symptom of my fear, or my doubts of the final victory.

Hitler wanted Britain to accept peace on Germany's terms, yet he received the British refusal of such an offer with almost disbelief. The possibility of surrender was formally rejected by Lord Halifax during a radio broadcast three days later, although the British had in fact already decided to fight some weeks before. Hitler's prior record in Europe suggested that he would fail to honour any pledges, while his treatment of those living in conquered territories was already evident to the whole world. Even if Britain could strike a deal to remain unconquered, the nation would inevitably suffer as a result, having to make large concessions to Germany and pay huge reparations. British interests were fundamentally incompatible with a Nazi Germany-controlled Europe.

Britain's refusal to meet Hitler's demands to end the war meant that the planning for Operation Sea Lion would continue. In the meantime, Hitler decided, a naval blockade and air attack would combine to destroy British resolve, and once morale had been suitably undermined, an invasion should simply be a mopping-up exercise. But the key deciding factor remained air superiority, for without control of the skies, German forces landing on the beaches would be bombed into obliteration and air attacks would similarly be repelled. The preconditions for an invasion would therefore depend on a contest of strength between the two rival air forces: the Royal Air Force's Fighter Command on one side, and the German Luftwaffe on the other. Everything would depend on the outcome.

(Right) Following Adolf Hitler's 'Last Appeal to Reason' speech of 19 July 1940, leaflets printed with highlights from the speech were dropped over Britain by German aircraft, in an unsuccessful attempt to encourage Britain to negotiate peace terms.

(Pages 44–45) Workmen carry part of the bullet-riddled fuselage of a Dornier Do 17, which had crashed over England. Shown alongside is the wreckage of many other crashed German aircraft stored at a scrapyard in Britain in August 1940.

A LAST APPEAL TO REASON

BY

ADOLF HITLER

Speech before the Reichstag, 19th July, 1940

I have summoned you to this meeting in the midst of our tremendous struggle for the freedom and the future of the German nation. I have done so, firstly, because I considered it imperative to give our own people an insight into the events, unique in history, that lie behind us, secondly, because I wished to express my gratitude to our magnificent soldiers, and thirdly, with the intention of appealing, once more and for the last time, to common sense in general.

If we compare the causes which prompted this historic struggle with the magnitude and the far-reaching effects of military events, we are forced to the conclusion that its general course and the sacrifices it has entailed are out of all proportion to the alleged reasons for its outbreak — unless they were nothing but a pretext for underlying intentions.

The programme of the National-Socialist Movement, in so far as it affected the future development of the Reich's relations with the rest of the world, was simply an attempt to bring about a definite revision of the Treaty of Versailles, though as far as at all possible, this was to be accomplished by peaceful means.

This revision was absolutely essential. The conditions imposed at Versailles were intolerable, not only, because of their humiliating discrimination and because the disarmament which they ensured deprived the German nation of all its rights, but far more so because of the consequent destruction of the material existence of one of the great civilized nations in the world, and the proposed annihilation of its future, the utterly senseless accumulation of immense tracts of territory under the domination of a number of States, the theft of all the irreparable foundations of life and indispensable vital necessities from a conquered nation. While this dictate was being drawn up, men of insight even among our foes were uttering warnings about the terrible consequences which the ruthless application of its insane conditions would entail — a proof that even among them the conviction predominated that such a dictate could not possibly be upheld in days to come. Their objections and protests were silenced by the assurance that the statutes of the newly-created League of Nations provided for a revision of these conditions; in fact, the League was supposed to be the competent authority. The hope of revision was thus at no time regarded as presumptuous, but as something natural. Unfortunately, the Geneva institution, as those responsible for Versailles had intended, never looked upon itself as a body competent to undertake any sensible revision, but from the very outset as nothing more than the guarantor of the ruthless enforcement and maintenance of the conditions imposed at Versailles.

All attempts made by democratic Germany to obtain equality for the German people by a revision of the Treaty proved unavailing.

World War Enemies Unscrupulous Victors

It is always in the interests of a conqueror to represent stipulations that are to his advantage as sacrosanct, while the instinct of self-preservation in the vanquished leads him to reacquire the common human rights that he has lost. For him the dictate of an overbearing conqueror had all the less legal force, since he had never been honourably conquered. Owing to a rare misfortune, the German Empire, between 1914 and 1918, lacked good leadership. To this, and to the as yet unenlightened faith and trust placed by the German people in the words of democratic statesmen, our downfall was due.

Hence the Franco-British claim that the Dictate of Versailles was a sort of international, or even a supreme, code of laws, appeared to be nothing more than a piece of insolent arrogance to every honest German, the assumption, however, that British or French statesmen should actually claim to be the guardians of justice, and even of human culture, as mere stupid effrontery. A piece of effrontery that is thrown into a sufficiently glaring light by their own extremely negligible achievements in this direction. For seldom have any countries in the world been ruled with a lesser degree of wisdom, morality and culture than those which are at the moment exposed to the ravings of certain democratic statesmen.

The programme of the National-Socialist Movement, besides freeing the Reich from the innermost fetters of a small substratum of Jewish-capitalistic and pluto-democratic profiteers, proclaimed to the world our resolution to shake off the shackles of the Versailles Dictate.

Germany's demands for this revision were a vital necessity and essential to the existence and honour of every great nation. They will probably one day be regarded by posterity as extremely reasonable. In practice, all these demands had to be carried through contrary to the will of the Franco-British rulers. We all regarded it as a sure sign of successful leadership in the Third Reich that for years we were able to effect this revision without a war. Not that — as the British and French demagogues asserted — we were at that time incapable of fighting. When, thanks to growing common sense, it finally appeared as though international co-operation might lead to a peaceful solution of the remaining problems, the Agreement to this end signed in Munich on September 29, 1938, by the four leading interested States, was not only not welcomed in London and Paris, but was actually condemned as a sign of abominable weakness. Now that peaceful revision threatened to be crowned with success, the Jewish capitalist war-mongers, their hands stained with blood, saw their tangible pretexts for realizing their diabolical plans vanish into thin air. Once again we witnessed a conspiracy by wretched corruptible political creatures and money-grabbing financial magnates, for whom war was a welcome means of furthering their business interests. The poison scattered by the ... throughout the nations began to exercise its disintegrating influence on sound common sense. Scribblers concentrated upon decrying honest men, who wanted peace, as weaklings and traitors, and upon denouncing the opposition parties as the Fifth Column, thus breaking all internal resistance to their criminal war policy. Jews and Freemasons, armaments manufacturers and war profiteers, international business-men and Stock Exchange jobbers seized upon political hirelings of the desperado and Herostrates type, who described war as something infinitely desirable.

It was the work of these criminal persons that spurred the Polish State on to adopt an attitude that was out of all proportion to Germany's demands and still less to the attendant consequences.

In its dealings with Poland, the German Reich has pre-eminently exercised genuine self-restraint since the National-Socialist régime came into power. One of the most despicable and foolish measures of the Versailles Dictate, namely, the severance of an old German province from the Reich, was crying out aloud for revision. Yet what were my requests?

I name myself in this connexion, because no other statesman might have dared to propose a solution such as mine to the German nation. It merely implied the return of Danzig — an ancient purely German city — to the Reich, and the creation of a means of communication between the Reich and its severed province. Even this was to be decided by a plebiscite subject to the control of an international body. If Mr Churchill and the rest of the war-mongers had felt a fraction of the responsibility towards Europe which inspired me, they could never have begun their infamous game.

It was only due to these and other European and non-European parties and their war interests, that Poland rejected my proposals, which in no way affected either her honour or her existence, and in their stead had recourse to terror and to the sword. In this case we once more showed unexampled and truly superhuman self-control, since for months, despite murderous attacks on minority Germans, and even despite the slaughter of tens of thousands of our German fellow-countrymen, we still sought an understanding by peaceful means.

What was the situation?

One of the most unnatural creations of the Dictate of Versailles, a popinjay puffed up with political and military pomp, insults another State for months on end and threatens to grind it to powder, to fight battles on the outskirts of Berlin, to hack the German armies to pieces, to extend its frontiers to the Oder or the Elbe, and so forth. Meanwhile, the other State, Germany, watches this tumult in patient silence, although a single movement of her arm would have sufficed to prick this bubble inflated with folly and hatred.

On September 2, the conflict might still have been averted — Mussolini proposed a plan for the immediate cessation of all hostilities and for peaceful negotiations. Though Germany saw her armies storming to victory, I nevertheless accepted his proposal. It was only the Franco-British war-mongers who desired war, not peace. More than that, as Mr Chamberlain said, they needed a long war, because they had now invested their capital in armaments shares, had purchased machinery and required time for the development of their business interests and the amortization of their investments. For, after all, what do these "citizens of the world" care about Poles, Czechs or such-like peoples?

On June 19, 1940, a German soldier found a curious document when searching some railway trucks standing in the station of La Charité. As the document bore a distinctive inscription, he immediately handed it over to his commanding officer. It was then passed on to other quarters, where it was soon realized that we had lighted on an important discovery. The station was subjected to another, more thorough-going search.

Thus it was that the German High Command gained possession of a collection of documents of unique historical significance. They were the secret documents of the Allied Supreme War Council, and included the minutes of every meeting held by this illustrious body. This time Mr Churchill will not succeed in contesting or lying about the veracity of these documents, as he tried to do when documents were discovered in Warsaw.

These documents bear marginal notes inscribed by Messieurs Gamelin, Daladier, Weygand, etc. They ran thus at any time ... consisted of related matters very good sense. They furnish remarkable evidence of the machinations of the war-mongers and war-extenders. Above all, they show that those stony-hearted politicians regarded all the small nations as a means to their ends; that they had attempted to use Finland in their own interests; that they had determined to turn Norway and Sweden into a theatre of war; that they had planned to fan a conflagration in the Balkans in order to gain the assistance of a hundred divisions from those countries; that they had planned a bombardment of Batum and Baku by a ruthless and unscrupulous interpretation of Turkey's neutrality, who was not unfavourable to them; that they had inveigled Belgium and the Netherlands more and more completely, until they finally entrapped them into binding General Staff agreements, and so on, ad libitum.

The documents further give a picture of the dilettante methods by which these political war-mongers tried to quench the blaze which they had lighted, of their democratic militarism, which is in part to blame for the appalling fate that they have inflicted on hundreds of thousands, even millions of their own soldiers, of their barbarous unscrupulousness which caused them callously to force mass evacuation on their peoples, which brought them no military advantages, though the effects on the population were outrageously cruel.

These same criminals are responsible for having driven Poland into war.

Eighteen days later this campaign was, to all intents and purposes, at an end.

Britain and France Considered Understanding a Crime

On October 6, 1939, I addressed the German nation for the second time during this war, this very place. I was able to inform them of our glorious military victory over the Polish State. At the same time I appealed to the insight of the responsible men in the enemy States and to the nations themselves. I warned them not to continue this war, the consequences of which could only be devastating. I particularly warned the French of embarking on a war which would forcibly eat its way across the frontier and which, irrespective of its outcome, would have appalling consequences. At the same time, I addressed this appeal to the rest of the world, although I feared — as I expressly said — that my words would not be heard, but would more than ever arouse the fury of the interested war-mongers. Everything happened as I predicted. The responsible elements in Britain and France scented in my appeal a dangerous attack on their war profits. They therefore immediately began to declare that every thought of conciliation was out of the question, nay, even a crime; that the war had to be pursued in the name of civilization, of humanity, of happiness, of progress, and — to leave no stone unturned — in the name of religion itself. For this purpose, negroes and bushmen were to be mobilized. Victory, they then said, would come of its own accord, it was, in fact, within their easy reach, as I myself must know very well and have known for a long time since, or I should not have broadcast my appeal for peace throughout the world. For if I had had any justification for

Chapter Two

THE OPPONENTS

By 1940, Germany's Luftwaffe was not only the largest air force in Europe but boasted a formidable reputation. Its commander-in-chief was Hermann Göring, Germany's air minister, who had been a fighter pilot ace during the First World War and was one of the founding members of the Nazi Party. The political power he had amassed by the beginning of the war had made him second only to Hitler in the Nazi chain of command, and as such the Luftwaffe was regarded by many as the most elite division of the German armed forces.

The average age of German pilots at the time of the Battle of Britain was twenty-six, although with a typical length of service of almost five years, most were well trained and combat experienced. Many, like Wolfgang Falck, had fought in the German Blitzkrieg attacks against Poland towards the end of the previous year.

> In Poland, I shot down three aircraft. The first one was a mixture of a fighter and dive-bomber. The second was a reconnaissance aircraft and the third was a three-engine Fokker aircraft. I remember getting the order to attack ground troops some distance behind the front and we saw a Polish battery with horses. We attacked them. I hated that – the poor horses. And I saw a big city burning for the first time – Warsaw. That was terrible. The German Air Force was greatly superior to the Polish Air Force. It didn't surprise me that victory came quickly. We had been so superior that we had compassion for the Polish people.

Pilots such as Falck were the cream of the Luftwaffe, a result of the high German standards of rigorous training. Indeed, this high benchmark would in due course contribute to a lack of pilots, as the time and work involved in training up replacements for those taken out of action was protracted, to say the least.

Unlike the RAF, which was organised into commands based on function, the Luftwaffe was arranged into self-contained air fleets (Luftflotten), which were formations complete with multiple varieties of aircraft including both fighters and bombers. Air Fleet 5 was based in Norway and operated long-range aircraft only; unacceptably high losses sustained in August 1940 would swiftly remove them from battle, and they were largely used for diversionary attacks against the north of Britain. The main air fleets operating in the Battle of Britain were therefore Air Fleet 2, commanded by Field Marshal Albert Kesselring, and Air Fleet 3, commanded by Field Marshal Hugo Sperrle. Air Fleet 2 was based at airfields in northern Germany, through Belgium and the Netherlands to Le Havre in France, and hosted a fighter squadron clustered around the Pas-de-Calais. Air Fleet 3 was also based in France but further to the west, and it was where bombers and dive bombers tended to be concentrated, for launching attacks on coastal areas and naval targets.

KEY PERSONALITY

Hermann Göring (1893–1946)
Commander-in-chief of the Luftwaffe

A decorated First World War fighter pilot, Göring was one of Adolf Hitler's closest political associates and his named successor. A long-standing member of the Nazi party, he held several senior posts in Hitler's government and was second only to the Führer in importance. His influence declined after the Luftwaffe's perceived failures, first in the Battle of Britain and then against the Soviet Union on the Eastern Front, as well as its inability to respond effectively to the Allied strategic bombing campaign later in the war. In the last weeks of the conflict, with Hitler trapped in an encircled Berlin, Göring sought authorisation to assume power and was denounced as a traitor. Following the German surrender in May 1945, he was arrested and became the highest-ranking Nazi to be tried for war crimes at Nuremberg. Convicted of crimes against humanity, he was sentenced to death, yet committed suicide on 15 October 1946, the night before his scheduled execution.

The defence of British airspace was the responsibility of the Royal Air Force. As we have already seen, the RAF experienced rapid development and expansion in the years before the outbreak of war, and this included the creation in 1936 of a specific Fighter Command under the direction of Air Chief Marshal Sir Hugh Dowding. Fighter Command was split into individual groups covering specific geographical areas of the country. The key ones involved in the Battle of Britain were 11 Group, covering London and much of south-east England (commanded by Air Vice-Marshal Keith Park), and 12 Group, covering the Midlands, East Anglia and parts of northern England (under Air Vice-Marshal Trafford Leigh-Mallory). Others, which would supply reinforcements as the battle progressed, included 13 Group, covering most of the north of England, Scotland and Northern Ireland, and 10 Group, covering Wales and south-west England.

The RAF could claim to be a truly international force. Of the almost 3,000 RAF and Fleet Air Arm aircrew involved in the Battle of Britain, only around 80 per cent were British. While Churchill's famous speech at the beginning of June referred to Britain 'fighting alone', this is not quite the case, since Fighter Command included men from all over the Empire and Commonwealth as well as occupied Europe. It could boast pilots from New Zealand, Australia, Canada, India, South Africa, Rhodesia (now Zimbabwe), Belgium, France, Poland and Czechoslovakia, not to mention some who originated from neutral countries such as the United States and Ireland. This international aspect extended to the commanding officers too, as 11 Group's Air Vice-Marshal Keith Park and 10 Group's Air Vice-Marshal Sir Quintin Brand were born in New Zealand and South Africa respectively.

The call went out to all corners of the British Empire that experienced pilots were needed to defend Britain. One of the first to respond from India was Mahinder Singh Pujji, who was originally from Simla and had taken up flying in 1936, aged eighteen, as a hobby at the Delhi Flying Club. He became a civil pilot with Himalayan Airlines and at the outbreak of war was employed as a refuelling superintendent at Shell Oil, but he still took the opportunity to fly wherever possible. Once news of the German attacks against Britain reached India, Pujji was among the first qualified pilots to respond to the patriotic call for airmen to help in the fight.

In 1940 I saw an ad in the newspaper saying that the RAF wanted qualified pilots. I immediately applied. My boss said that he would keep my job, and within a month, I was in England. Twenty-four qualified pilots arrived together at Liverpool and we were all commissioned on August 1 as pilot officers. We arrived in London and we were billeted in temporary huts in Uxbridge. We could see the searchlights looking for the German aircraft and I was longing to fly. When we arrived, we met a lot of people and I appreciated the spirit of Londoners. They were very friendly and courageous. It fascinated me that the people were so brave.

KEY PERSONALITY

Field Marshal Albert Kesselring
(1885–1960), Commander of Air Fleet 2

A career army officer, Kesselring enlisted in 1904 and served on the Western Front during the First World War. In 1933 he was given an administrative post in the Luftwaffe and, at the age of 48, learned to fly. Originally given command of Air Fleet 1 during the invasion of Poland, he took over Air Fleet 2 in May 1940 ahead of the campaigns against France, Belgium, the Netherlands and Luxembourg. Kesselring remained in command during the Battle of Britain and his air fleet carried out the main weight of attacks against south-east England. He was also instrumental in making the decision in September 1940 to switch from attacking airfields to targeting London and other major cities. This critical error of judgement put Kesselring further at odds with the commander of Air Fleet 3, Hugo Sperrle. After the Battle of Britain, Kesselring's air fleet went on to support the Germany Army during the invasion of the Soviet Union. While Kesselring's Allied opponents respected him for his military achievements, his record also included atrocities committed on his orders in Italy; he subsequently faced trial at Nuremberg and received a death sentence, which was commuted to life imprisonment. He was released in 1952, ostensibly on health grounds, only a few years before his death.

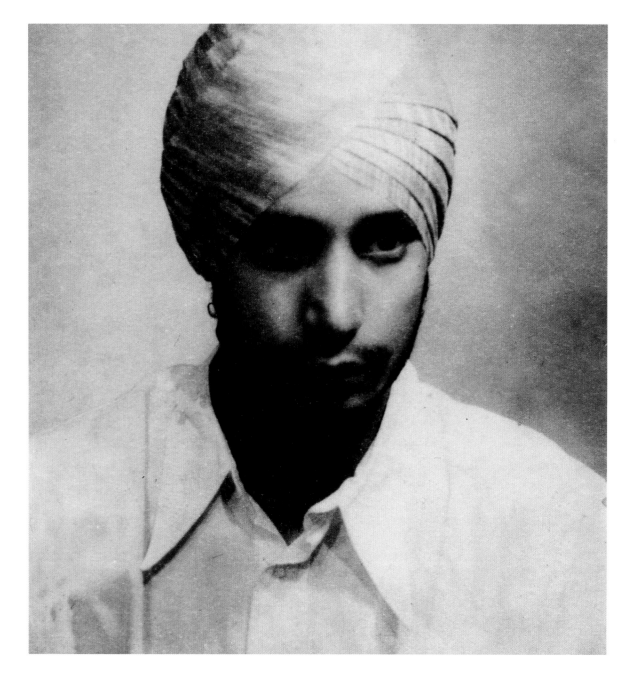

Squadron Leader Mahinder Singh Pujji at the age
of 19. He was already a qualified pilot and was
employed by the Shell Oil Company to supervise
the refuelling of flying boats.

(Page 46–47) Adolf Hitler and Admiral Erich
Raeder in discussion at the map table during a
planning conference at the Berghof, July 1940.
Also present are (left to right) Field Marshal
Walther von Brauchitsch, General Alfred Jodl,
Field Marshal Wilhelm Keitel and an unidentified
Kriegsmarine staff officer.

(Page 52–53) Hermann Göring (1893–1946), the
Luftwaffe commander-in-chief, addresses a group
of German pilots during the Battle of Britain.

Portrait photograph of Major Wolfgang Falck, who commanded the Luftwaffe's first dedicated night fighter unit, Nachtjagdgeschwader (NJG) 1, until 1943. Falck was instrumental, along with General Josef Kammhuber, in creating Nazi Germany's highly efficient night fighter force.

Major Werner Mölders and Major Adolf Galland,
two leading fighter aces of the Luftwaffe during
the Battle of Britain, in conversation with
Reichsmarschall Hermann Göring (centre) on
the French coast, 1940.

A Supermarine Spitfire of No. 19 Squadron
RAF being rearmed between sorties at Fowlmere,
Cambridgeshire, in September 1940.

There wasn't any prejudice in London, but on our way to London we'd called in at Durban and Cape Town in South Africa. While we were in Cape Town, my friends and I were having dinner, dressed in our RAF uniforms, when the waiter came along and said, 'Are you from Egypt?' 'No,' we said, 'we're from India.' He looked shocked and he went away. After about half an hour, the manager came and said, 'I'm sorry, I'm not allowed to serve people from your country.' Among us there were two or three experienced pilots of international repute. They were furious. 'What do you think?' they said. 'We have come here to fight for the British and that's what you're telling us?' One pilot got very angry and hit the glass table with his shoe and broke it into pieces. A scene was created and very soon there were police and officers, and after an hour, they apologised to us and we were taken back to our hotel where it was explained that the prejudice was a local South African thing and not a British thing. But South Africa was under British rule.

The Indian airmen would undoubtedly have expected similar treatment on arrival in Britain itself, although they were actually in line for a pleasant surprise.

We didn't see any of this prejudice in Britain at all... Everyone was nice to us. Those of us in turbans were the special VIPs for everybody because we looked very strange with the RAF wings on our turbans. We got VIP treatment in restaurants. There were no eggs and no sugar available, but when we asked for them they were produced from somewhere or other. They wanted to oblige us.

Throughout my air force career I was allowed to wear my turban. I made a special request to the RAF that I didn't want to take off my turban to fly. They were curious because there were other Sikh pilots who readily took off their turbans and put on helmets. But I told them that I didn't want to because of my religion. So they allowed me to have a special headset with the oxygen mask and microphone that came over the turban. The British were very accommodating.

Other pilots joined the fight from European countries which had already fallen to the Nazis. Ludwik Martel had managed to escape to France during the fall of Poland, before making his way to Britain, where he would be welcomed into the RAF. Many airmen like Martel felt that they had not had the opportunity to properly engage with the enemy in the face of the sudden German Blitzkrieg invasions of their homelands.

The beginning of the war in Poland was very sudden. I was called in and reported to my unit in Poznan on September 1, 1939. The first German bomb came down as I left the train. From then onwards we were more or less running away from the bombers. We were

KEY PERSONALITY

Field Marshal Hugo Sperrle
(1885–1953), Commander of Air Fleet 3

Sperrle joined the Imperial German Army's air arm in 1914 and, training as a pilot, became involved with aerial reconnaissance during the First World War. In 1934 he was promoted and formally transferred to the Luftwaffe, and in 1936 he was given command of the Condor Legion with which he would fight in the Spanish Civil War. The Legion attracted global controversy for its involvement in the bombing of civilians, most infamously at Guernica. Shortly before the outbreak of the Second World War, Sperrle was appointed to command Air Fleet 3, and his squadrons played a crucial role in the invasion of France and subsequently the Battle of Britain; his direction of bombing operations over London and the south-east was particularly important. Despite having limited experience of flying, Sperrle proved to be a popular leader who brought with him vital organisational skills and a valuable understanding of operations. From the middle of 1941, Air Fleet 3 took on the main defence of German-occupied western Europe, yet the combined Allied bomber offensive meant that Sperrle's force had become seriously depleted by mid-1944 and was unable to stop the Allied landings in Normandy on D-Day. As a direct consequence, Sperrle was dismissed from senior command. He was arrested at the end of the war and faced trial for war crimes, but was acquitted.

Major Adolf Galland, Geschwaderkommodore of JG 26, photographed with his dog 'Schweinebauch' at Audembert, France, in 1940.

attacked and bombed without heart. They were just bombing every possible target with people running away from their homes... As a reservist, I joined a unit who were going to collect aircraft from Romania. But when we reached the border on September 17, the unit was more or less disbanded. That was a very unpleasant time because we realised that everything was gone, it was finished, and we had to look ahead to join the fighting in the west. I felt full of hatred. I wanted to fly and to be able to shoot the opposition. I went to France but I had a very unpleasant experience in France. As soon as the agreement between the British government and the Polish government was made, I came to England. It was a very pleasant surprise when we were allowed to go flying in England. We got access to modern equipment, which I had been dreaming of. In England, I went through preliminary training and got familiar with aviation in the west because, after all, it had been nearly six months since I left Poland and had been near aircraft. I was very pleased when after fifty minutes training on a Spitfire, I was posted to a Spitfire squadron.

Alan Deere recalled how the shortage of pilots early on during the Battle of Britain meant that the air force used air crew who could claim little flying experience.

We were getting pilots who had not been on Spitfires because there were no conversion units at that time. They came straight to a squadron from their training establishments. Some of them did have a few hours on the Hurricanes, a monoplane experience, but not on the Spitfire. For example, we got two young New Zealanders into my flight. Chatting to them, I found they'd been six weeks at sea coming over. They were trained on some very outdated aircraft, I can't remember, out in New Zealand. They were given I think two trips or something in a Hurricane, something of that sort of order, and they arrived at the squadron. We were pretty busy and so we gave them what was known as a cockpit check. We had by that time a monoplane and we'd give them one trip in that. One of the pilots would take them up to see the handling and brief them on the Spitfire. Then they'd go off for one solo flight and circuit, and then they were into battle. The answer is, of course, that they didn't last. Those two lasted two trips and they both finished up in Dover Hospital, strangely enough. One was pulled out of the Channel. One landed by parachute.

One such 'sprog' (as the recently qualified pilots were often described by their more experienced colleagues) was Jimmy Corbin.

After you'd done a few hours flying and done a bit of formation flying either with two or three or maybe more, and then eventually with the squadron, then they called you operational: that meant you were fit to be killed! The first aerobatics I did was in a Spitfire. I was

KEY PERSONALITY

Air Chief Marshal Sir Hugh Dowding

(1882–1970), commander-in-chief of RAF Fighter Command

Dowding oversaw the defence of Britain in the summer and autumn of 1940. He was a career airman, having first joined the Royal Flying Corps (later the Royal Air Force) at the start of the First World War. In 1936 he was appointed head of Fighter Command and he spearheaded the development of the air defence network that gave the RAF such a critical advantage during the Battle of Britain. Dowding was 58 years old at the start of the battle, the oldest of the RAF's senior commanders, and nearing the end of his career; although he had been scheduled to retire in July 1940, this had been delayed at the request of the chief of air staff, Sir Cyril Newall. Dowding played a central role in directing British defences throughout the battle. Although he was viewed by many as stubborn and difficult to work with, no one had a better grasp of how to run Britain's defence system or manage Fighter Command's precious and relatively limited resources of both men and aircraft. But as the summer and autumn of 1940 wore on, Dowding found himself increasingly at odds with some of his subordinates, as well as senior officials at the Air Ministry, and he was replaced in November. After a short period at the Ministry of Aircraft Production, he finally retired in July 1942.

told by the squadron commander, 'Corbin! There's your aircraft, go and do one hour's aerobatic flying.' I thought, 'Christ almighty! I've never done any aerobatic flying.' So I thought the loop must be the easiest thing. Of course, in my bloody ignorance and stupidity I went up in this loop and I stalled the bloody thing at the top through going around too fast; it spun out the top...! That was my first experience.

In order to accommodate the significant number of pilots who had arrived in Britain from occupied Europe, the War Cabinet created two Polish fighter squadrons, Nos. 302 and 303, in early July 1940. These were followed by other national units, including a Canadian squadron and two fighter squadrons comprising pilots from Czechoslovakia. The highest scoring pilot of the Battle of Britain was in fact Josef Frantisek, a Czech pilot flying with No. 303 (Polish) Fighter Squadron. This particular unit entered the battle on 31 August, at the peak of the Battle of Britain, but quickly became Fighter Command's highest-claiming squadron with 126 kills.

All of the pilots fighting for Britain were famously referred to by Churchill as 'The Few' in a speech to Parliament on 20 August.

> The great air battle which has been in progress over this Island for the last few weeks has recently attained a high intensity. We must certainly expect that greater efforts will be made by the enemy than any he has so far put forth... The gratitude of every home in our Island, in our Empire, and indeed throughout the world, except in the abodes of the guilty, goes out to the British airmen who, undaunted by odds, unwearied in their constant challenge and mortal danger, are turning the tide of the world war by their prowess and by their devotion. Never in the field of human conflict was so much owed by so many to so few. All hearts go out to the fighter pilots, whose brilliant actions we see with our own eyes day after day.

The prime minister chose his words to deliberately reinforce the notion that the German pilots heavily outnumbered the British. But this was far from being the case: on 27 July 1940 the operational pilot strength of Fighter Command was 1,377 compared to 869 for the Germans (equivalent count from roughly the same date). The statistics for the number of operational aircraft also indicate a British advantage. On 10 August 1940 the Germans had 1,011 operational single-engine fighter aircraft assigned to the Battle of Britain, slightly fewer than the equivalent figure for Fighter Command. Britain would suffer from shortages of non-combat personnel and ground crew throughout the battle, yet all that the British could do in the time available was put in extra effort to make up for the deficiency in numbers – as Churchill put it, to simply 'work faster'.

Air Vice-Marshal Keith Park
(1892–1975), commander of 11 Group, RAF Fighter Command

Park oversaw the RAF's 11 Group, which covered London and the south-east and suffered most heavily during the Battle of Britain. He had previously served as senior air staff officer to Dowding, who maintained a deep respect for Park. Keith Park was a tough leader, well liked and highly respected by the men under his command, yet he often clashed with other members of the RAF leadership. He had a particularly abrasive relationship with the commander of 12 Group, Air Vice-Marshal Trafford Leigh-Mallory, who was a key supporter of the controversial 'Big Wing' tactic: this involved deploying a large formation of fighters to intercept incoming German bombers, but getting such a great number of aircraft airborne took time and Park's fighters in the hard-hit 11 Group were left vulnerable by the delay. In December 1940, Park was replaced by Leigh-Mallory and Park transferred to RAF Training Command. He was later appointed air officer commanding in Malta, where he organised the air defence of the heavily besieged island (in 1942 he would receive a knighthood for his crucial role in Malta's defence). He continued to hold a number of senior positions in the RAF, ending the war as Allied air commander-in-chief of South East Asia Command.

A pilot of No. 242 Squadron RAF photographed in full flying kit, wearing his oxygen mask and standing on the wing of a Hurricane at Duxford, Cambridgeshire, in September 1940.

(Right) Sergeant M Eriksen of the Royal Norwegian Air Force Serving with the RAF by Eric Kennington, 1942.

A group of pilots of No. 303 (Polish) Squadron RAF at Leconfield, North Yorkshire, on 24 October 1940. Shown (left to right) are Pilot Officer Bogusław Mierzwa, Pilot Officer Witold 'Tolo' Łokuciewski, Pilot Officer Mirosław 'Ox' Ferić, Flight Lieutenant John A Kent 'Kentowski', Flying Officer Bogdan Grzeszczak, Pilot Officer Jan 'Donald Duck' Zumbach, Pilot Officer Jerzy Radomski, Flying Officer Zdzisław Henneberg and Sergeant Eugeniusz Szaposznikow.

A posed photograph of pilots from No. 312 (Czech) Squadron RAF in flying kit 'sprinting' to their Hurricanes at Duxford, Cambridgeshire, in September 1940.

Hurricane pilots of No. 111 Squadron RAF relax
with a pet dog outside their caravan at Wick,
Scotland, in April 1940.

(Left) Pilots from No. 66 Squadron RAF wait
in readiness in their crew room at Duxford,
Cambridgeshire. Shown are Flying Officer R F
Rimmer, Flight Sergeant Jones, Pilot Officer R W
'Bobby' Oxspring and Flying Officer Brown.

(Page 68) Boulton Paul Defiant pilots and gunners
of No. 264 Squadron RAF play a game of draughts
while waiting at readiness outside their dispersal
tent at Kirton in Lincolnshire, August 1940.

The Battle of Britain A Visual History

Air Vice-Marshal Trafford Leigh-Mallory (1892–1944), commander of 12 Group, RAF Fighter Command

Leigh-Mallory served as a pilot with the Royal Flying Corps during the First World War, and was ultimately placed in command of an RAF squadron. Having chosen to pursue a career in the RAF, he had received a promotion to command 12 Group at the outbreak of the Second World War and was responsible for the area of Fighter Command to the north of London. As one of the younger air vice-marshals serving with the RAF he proved popular among his staff, although relations with the commanders of individual airfields could often be strained. He quarrelled in particular with the commander of 11 Group, Air Vice-Marshal Keith Park, as well as Sir Hugh Dowding, criticising their lack of support for the 'Big Wing' strategy of using large fighter squadrons to hunt down enemy bomber formations. Some believed that Leigh-Mallory conspired to have both Park and Dowding removed from their posts. He took over from Park as commander of 11 Group in December 1940 shortly after the Battle of Britain had ended and became commander-in-chief of RAF Fighter Command in 1942, before being promoted to oversee the combined Allied air forces for the D-Day invasion. While he was en route to Ceylon to take up the post of air commander-in-chief of South East Asia Command, Leigh-Mallory's aircraft crashed in the French Alps, killing him along with his wife and eight others. He was one of the most senior British officers to lose his life during the war.

In this photograph taken on 24 October 1940, a score of 126 enemy aircraft shot down by No. 303 (Polish) Squadron RAF during the Battle of Britain has been chalked on the fuselage of a Hurricane at Leconfield, North Yorkshire.

Pilots of 'B' Flight, No. 32 Squadron RAF relax on the grass at Hawkinge in Kent, in front of a Hurricane. Shown (from left to right) are Pilot Officer R F Smythe, Pilot Officer K R Gillman, Pilot Officer J E Proctor, Flight Lieutenant P M Brothers, Pilot Officer D H Grice, Pilot Officer P M Gardner and Pilot Officer A F Eckford. All survived the war, except Keith Gillman, who was posted as missing on 25 August 1940.

However, it was certainly true that the RAF were often outnumbered in terms of individual engagements. The Luftwaffe concentrated their attacks over the south of England while Fighter Command was spread across the country. In addition, the fight was also often unequal in terms of aircraft type, with British fighter squadrons regularly facing multiple groups of enemy bombers and larger fighters, as well as the standard fighter escorts. To that extent, at least, the idea of 'The Few' remains an accurate interpretation. As an aside, it is also important to remember that at the time of the battle, Britain didn't realise the true state of German pilot strength, with their intelligence sources overestimating the size of the opposition to a very significant degree. This expectation of a seriously overwhelming battle therefore acted in Britain's favour, by encouraging a higher scale of preparation and commitment than might otherwise have been the case.

As well as the number of pilots and air crew available to each respective air force, another key factor which would determine the result of the Battle of Britain was the aircraft production capacity of each opponent. While the loss of any aircraft was an obvious concern, the ability to replace them at a regular and efficient rate was even more important. Aircraft production was boosted in Britain throughout 1940, particularly during the summer months, when the battle was at its height. Preparations for an increased production rate had already been made some time before, yet the new appointment of Lord Beaverbrook as minister of aircraft production in May 1940 brought his energy and experience as one of the country's leading newspaper publishers to bear on the issue. In January 1940 the British government had set a target of some 3,602 fighter aircraft, and this was easily met and surpassed: actual production would reach 4,283 over the course of the year. This success was in spite of the fact that the RAF was actually fighting on two fronts, and therefore needed to supply aircraft for the war in the Middle East as well as for the defence of Britain. Only 509 aircraft in total were imported from overseas, and half of these arrived from late September onwards, when the Battle of Britain was almost over; Britain therefore had to rely on its own production capabilities more than anything else. In this sense, the nation was very much 'fighting alone'.

By comparison, German aircraft production remained sluggish throughout 1940. At the start of the war Hitler had planned to double production, but the country's aircraft industry had to reduce targets on a regular basis as factories struggled to meet their planned numbers. The production of single-engine fighters in Germany reached only 1,870 during the whole of 1940; Britain managed to produce 2,091 in only half that time. But why should there have been such low production figures when German aviation was one of the leading industries in the world and enjoyed a huge amount of resourcing? One explanation is that their head of air force procurement was the weak Colonel Ernst Udet who, easily manipulated and misled by other German businessmen and officials, proved an inefficient leader before

Squadron Leader Douglas Bader
(1910–1982), commander of No. 242 Squadron RAF

At the outbreak of war in 1939, Douglas Bader set out to rejoin the RAF. He had been discharged from the service six years previously after losing both his legs in a flying accident while taking part in an aerobatics display. Within six months, he had been fitted with artificial legs and learned to walk again. He was able to persuade the RAF to give him a chance to prove that he could still fly operationally and he joined No. 19 Squadron, based at RAF Duxford in Cambridgeshire, in early 1940. Bader was soon made a flight commander of No. 222 Squadron, and he took part in the Battle of France in May and June 1940 during which he shot down several German aircraft. He was then posted to command No. 242 Squadron at RAF Coltishall, with whom he served throughout the Battle of Britain. Bader was an aggressive pilot and over the next few months would shoot down many enemy aircraft; he was awarded a Distinguished Service Order in September 1940 for his combat leadership. Bader was a key supporter of the 'Big Wing' tactic and led the 'Duxford Wing' against German bombers. He was shot down over France on 9 August 1941 and spent the rest of the war in captivity. He remained well known as a personality after the war, largely due to *Reach for the Sky*, a biographical book (1954) and film (1956). In 1976 he was knighted for his services to disabled people.

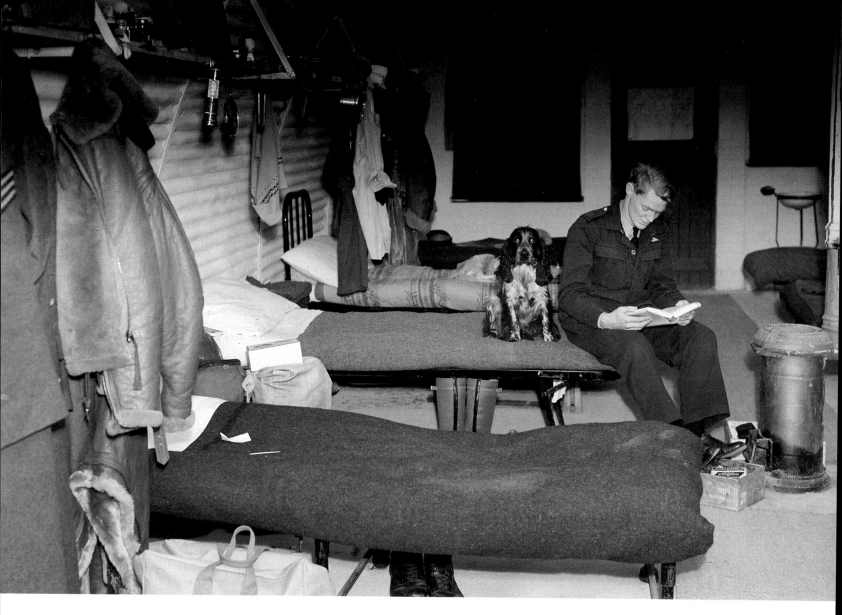

Flying Officer Frank Brinsden of No. 19 Squadron RAF sits on a bed in the pilots' quarters at Fowlmere, Cambridgeshire, in September 1940.

he committed suicide in 1941. Another factor limiting production was the nature of the German aircraft themselves: their technical complexity made them very difficult to build at speed.

Despite these differences, in many ways the two opposing forces of the RAF and Luftwaffe were evenly matched. Both were well-developed air forces which could boast the newest technology, high numbers of well-trained and experienced pilots, and commanders of experience and renown. But the course of the Battle of Britain would see certain advantages develop which would tip the scale enough to make a difference to the final outcome.

Chapter Three

THE INITIAL PHASE,
JUNE–JULY 1940

Many histories of the Battle of Britain give the official start of the battle as 10 July 1940, and that particular date was chosen to mark the earliest eligibility for individuals claiming the Battle of Britain medal clasp. But it could, in fact, be argued that the Battle of Britain began some weeks earlier, albeit in a gradual way, almost immediately after the evacuations from Dunkirk and elsewhere in France at the very beginning of June. The night of 5/6 June had seen minor bombing raids by the Luftwaffe begin over England, largely classed as 'nuisance raids', and these would continue in an infrequent, sporadic way throughout June and July 1940.

Through these raids, German fighters began to probe Fighter Command's defensive shield around south-eastern Britain, undertaking regular hit-and-run attacks against widely scattered targets in an attempt to test British resolve. Large formations of German fighters protected much smaller groups of German bombers or dive bombers. The German bombers were essentially intended as bait to attract the British fighters, which were the real target; an engagement would then follow with the German fighter escorts. The Luftwaffe concentrated on coastal targets by day, but at night roamed over much of southern Britain. These missions were largely uneventful, resulting in little serious destruction or loss of life either on the ground or in the air. They did result in regular sustained losses by the Luftwaffe themselves, though, which indicated how the Battle of Britain would develop over the next few months – essentially, as a war of attrition.

Fighter Command squadrons soon got used to the daily routine, with pilots and aircrew waiting for the moment when they were called into action – 'scrambled' – and would take to their aircraft to engage with the enemy. Denys Gillam was a Spitfire pilot with No. 616 Squadron RAF, based in South Yorkshire, and he vividly recalled how the regular routine could lead to serious fatigue.

> One was called about four in the morning and you went down to dispersal in the half light, and breakfast was brought down... And then you generally scrambled about seven or eight o'clock for the first raid. And then you came back, refuelled and rearmed, and they brought sandwiches down to one at the dispersal. And then you got scrambled again and had another battle, and probably a third in the afternoon or evening. And then towards dusk you would ease up and you were on readiness until just after dark. At the end of our tour, when there were only three or four of us, they were even asking us to night fly, which was very hard because we really weren't getting enough sleep. And this was very hard. In fact one night I went off after a raid and I think I went to sleep in the cockpit, because the next thing I knew, the speed was building up and there were lights in front of me, and I couldn't make out what it was and I realised I was upside down and diving hard to the ground. And this was entirely due to fatigue. I think the evening raid was the worst in

(Right) *Corporal J D M Pearson GC, WAAF* by Laura Knight, 1940. Daphne Pearson was serving as a WAAF medical orderly at Detling airfield in Kent when an Avro Anson bomber crashed upon landing on 31 May 1940. Her selfless rescue of the crew led to her receipt of the George Cross, the highest award for gallantry not in the direct presence of the enemy.

(Pages 74–75) *Air Fight over Portland* by Richard Eurich, 1940.

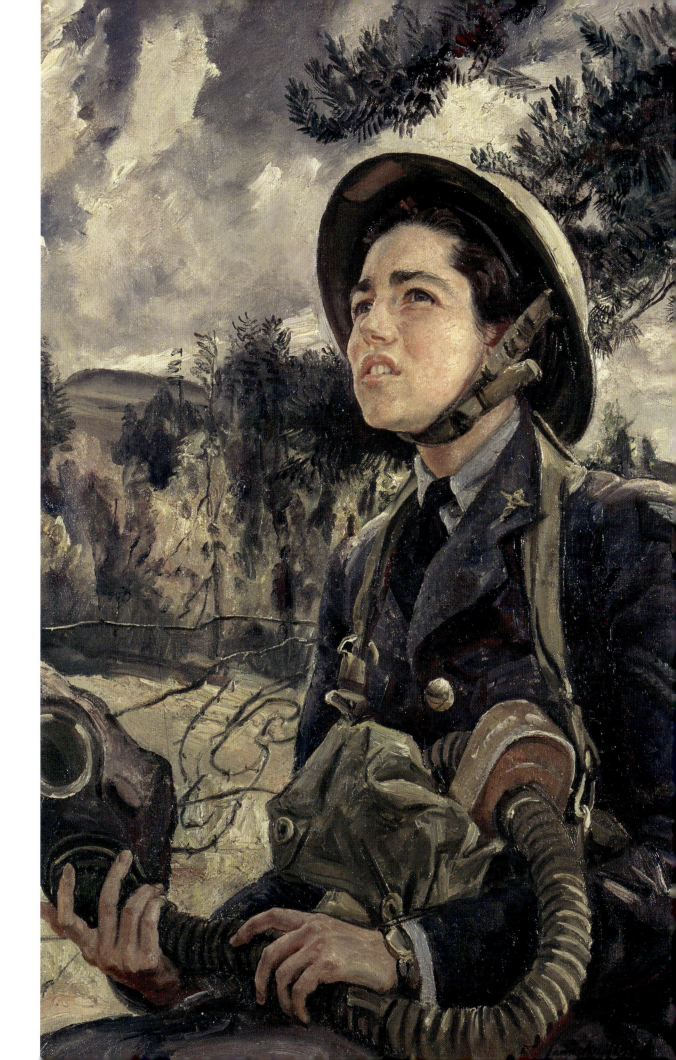

Prime Minister Winston Churchill meets
infantrymen manning a coastal defence
position near Hartlepool, County Durham,
during inspections on 31 July 1940.

A crowd of bystanders gathers around the wreckage of a Junkers Ju 88A which crashed at Oakridge, near Stroud in Gloucestershire. The bomber was attempting to attack the Gloster aircraft plant at Hucclecote on 25 July 1940 when it collided with a British aircraft.

that one had already flown three or four sorties and probably lost three or four pilots, and you were reduced down in numbers. Then you had another go and one was getting tired.

This first phase of the Battle of Britain could be characterised as a learning opportunity for both sides, as the RAF and Luftwaffe began to take stock of each other's capabilities and tactics. Throughout this period, anti-aircraft artillery units also undertook a lot of valuable practice. Second Lieutenant Cyril Sherwood, who served with the 91st Heavy Anti-Aircraft Regiment of the Royal Artillery, described how such gun crews operated.

> The 3.7-inch anti-aircraft guns had ten to a dozen people on the crew. There was a gun position officer in charge. There was a range finder which worked out the range and a predictor which followed the course of the plane and predicted where the plane would be when the shell reached a particular point. There were people on the gun traversing and elevating the gun, setting the fuse on the shell, loading the shell on the tray, ramming it home and firing.

> The predictor told us the right point to fire. If a bomber is weaving about, there's not a hope in hell of being able to hit it, but there's a period when it has to do a run-up: it flies at the same height, the same speed and in the same direction so that the bomb aimer can drop his bombs accurately. That run-up was the period when you could perhaps hit the plane, and that was the period when the predictor used to follow the plane through telescopes, and according to the rate of change of the bearing, you could get an idea of where the plane would be when a shell exploded. The shell had a fuse at the front which was set to a particular time, for example six seconds, and it would explode at a particular height. Theoretically, the plane and the shell would be at the same point. It was an almost impossible job. The best you could hope to do was to get the shells near enough to deter the plane so it moved off, making the bomb aiming less accurate.

Such was the theory, yet in practice the chances of hitting an enemy aircraft with anti-aircraft fire were relatively slim. Fighter aircraft such as the Hurricanes or Spitfires tended to prove much more effective as a deterrent. J W Clark was an anti-aircraft gunner based near Dover who recorded an interesting encounter in his diary entry for Friday, 5 July.

> Lots of alarms last night, some for very high flying planes. There was one at 5.30am and soon a plane went over us, then returned. Cloud was thick and then we saw him, a Heinkel 111, at 9,500 feet. D4 opened first and we followed at once, but Jerry popped in and out of the clouds and made things difficult. Then a Spitfire arrived, and we heard three bursts of machine guns. The planes circled away from us towards Folkestone, then out to sea, finally coming into sight

A sergeant air gunner inspects the number of 'kills' painted on the tail fin of a shot-down Messerschmitt Bf 109, now stored in an RAF hangar. The aircraft had been piloted by Oberleutnant Franz von Werra and crash-landed on 5 September 1940 at Winchet Hill, near Marden in Kent.

much lower, about 4,000 feet. Then the fighter administered the coup-de-grâce with a zooming attack from below and the Heinkel turned straight towards us and crashed under the cliffs. Loud cheers from the troops and triumphant stunts from the pilot.

Two of the crew, the only survivors, were brought up to our camp. One was a brawny, truculent youth, the traditional type of German, and the other slightly built and dark, with black hair brushed straight back. He may have been Austrian. They were given breakfast and were surprised to see sugar in a bowl, and still more surprised by apparently unlimited cigarettes. While their clothes were drying in the cookhouse the shoulder badges vanished, and there was a considerable fuss about it. The souvenir hunters had to give them up.

This Heinkel had been on a reconnaissance flight up to the outskirts of London, and along the north Kent coast. Only at Dover had he run into AA [anti-aircraft] fire or even any fighters. Some of our shots were close enough to cause slight shrapnel wounds in the pilot's legs and backside, but it was the Spitfire that fetched him down. The two Huns were quite ready to talk.

While these weeks gave both sides valuable experience, it is probably fair to say that the defenders gained much more than the attackers. Any hopes that Hitler may have had that Britain would give up immediately were dashed. Fighter Command worked hard to make sure that their squadrons were able to get airborne quickly, while deploying their aircraft in an economical way. Over time they would also adopt greater flexibility in flying strategy, using smaller formations to engage the enemy in case such attacks proved to be feints. This helped to conserve resources, though there were some unfortunate instances of unequal aerial battles in which Spitfires or Hurricanes were hugely outnumbered.

Fighter Command also adapted their strategy to the specific threat posed by the German bombers. While the Luftwaffe intended their bombers to attack ground targets while their fighters picked off the British aircraft in separate engagements, Fighter Command made it their priority to tackle the bombers first, as the main threat. The consequence of this decision was that the German fighters had to remain in close proximity to the bombers in order to protect them, which reduced their own combat flexibility. The successful German tactic of flying fighters in pairs, with one protecting the other, was therefore frustrated to a great extent. Yet the numbers of Luftwaffe aircraft in the skies, even at this early point of the battle, meant that any engagements could easily prove lethal. Hugh Ironside was a pilot with No. 151 Squadron RAF.

(Pages 82–83) A little girl donates money to a nurse collecting for the Red Cross in front of a Messerschmitt Bf 109 on display to the public at Fairfield car park in Croydon, August 1940. This particular aircraft was flown by Oberleutnant Bartels and shot down by Spitfires on 24 July 1940.

Hawker Hurricanes of No. 32 Squadron
RAF photographed at Hawkinge in Kent,
29 July 1940.

A Hawker Hurricane flown by Squadron Leader
Peter Townsend, the commanding officer of No.
85 Squadron RAF, being refuelled at Castle Camps,
Cambridgeshire, in July 1940.

A group of civilians and RAF airmen inspect the burning remains of a Heinkel He 111 which was shot down by RAF fighters over the north-east coast of Scotland and crashed on a house in July 1940.

On July 9 we were scrambled to patrol a convoy in the Thames Estuary. The convoy had been through the Channel and was on its way up north... someone said, 'Tally ho!' and we saw a great mass of German aircraft coming over. The bombers were below and the fighters, Messerschmitt 109s and 110s, were up above them. There were about 70 or 80 aircraft. As we went flat out into them, the 110s formed a circle. The 110s always formed a circle where they covered each other's tails. Our idea was to burst through the circle and get to the bombers underneath. From my point of view that didn't work out, because I got shot. I don't know where it came from, but it blew the windscreen away. I couldn't see anything – my eyes were full of bits of glass. The only thing to do was bail out, because I couldn't land the bloody thing if I couldn't see. I was tugging away at the hood to try and get it open but it wouldn't. There was no hope then for bailing out, but luckily one of my eyes cleared and I flew towards North Weald. I had no undercarriage, no lights, no radio and very little in the way of instruments, so I flew over the control tower, waggling my wings to ask if the undercarriage was down, which fortunately it was, and I landed.

George Unwin was equally as lucky, after an aerial duel with a German aircraft left his fighter seriously damaged.

I was at about 20,000 feet and I suddenly saw this lone Dornier; how he was on his own I'll never know, but he was off home. So I went after him. Now the drill against the Dornier was that he had a dustbin rear gunner, a dustbin hanging down below the fuselage, and you had to fix him first and then close in for the aircraft. This I did cleverly of course. I could see him shooting at me and I closed in and gave him a burst and shut him up, at least I thought I had. I never know to this day whether I did or I didn't or whether someone took his place, because as I closed right in on him and started shooting, I suddenly saw his rear gunner shooting back at me with little red sparks – you can see. I didn't pay much attention to it, I just thought he would stop another one and carried on firing for quite a while, quite a long burst, when suddenly I was covered in smoke. To my horror a hole appeared; I was leaning forward of course, as one did, to the gun-sight and a hole appeared in this thing in front of my face. I thought, 'Good God, I must be dead or something, no blood, no nothing but I'm covered in smoke.' I thought I was on fire.

So I whipped the hood back, undid my straps and started to get out. By this time I'd broken away and was going downhill. And I was halfway out of the cockpit when I suddenly saw that smoke was coming from the top of the engine, through the engine cowling, which is where the glycol pipe is, the coolant pipe. It was a really browny colour, it wasn't black smoke, and I could smell it too; it was glycol. So I got back in and strapped myself in again, left the hood

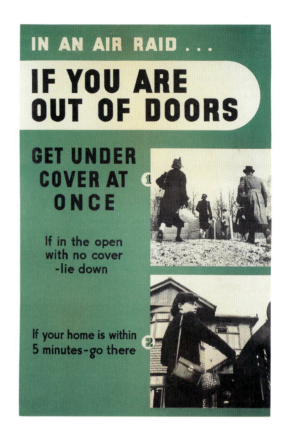

The British government issued many advisory posters to explain what people should do in the event of enemy air raids. While public or home shelters were the best option, it was quite possible to be caught outside during a daylight bombing raid without any obvious protection.

Gunners of 177 Heavy Battery, Royal Artillery, man an anti-aircraft Lewis gun at Fort Crosby near Liverpool on 1 August 1940. Such weaponry was of rather limited value against aircraft and was more likely to be used during anti-invasion operations.

(Pages 92–93) Soldiers collecting for the Spitfire Fund use the fuselage of a crashed Heinkel He 111 as a focus of interest for locals in a street 'somewhere in south-east England', 10 October 1940. Launched by Lord Beaverbrook, the fund raised money from public donations to build some 1,500 aircraft.

open and still went rapidly downhill in case somebody was following me, and then started looking for a field and I found a field to land in. I waited until I'd found my field and got down to about 1,000 feet, dropped the undercarriage and did a forced landing in this field no trouble at all.

I hadn't even got out of the cockpit before an army jeep with a young subaltern and two soldiers with fixed bayonets came roaring through the gate in a jeep, and as soon as they saw it was one of ours they changed their attitude. I got a screwdriver from one of the soldiers and we took the top off and there it was: a bullet had gone through the glycol pipe, the top – the header; there was glycol all over the place.

From the perspective of the Luftwaffe, there was some confusion over the exact instructions issued to them. On 17 July the air force were ordered 'to full readiness' and they began to attack ports and shipping in a more systematic way as part of the blockade operation. But a separate directive issued the day before had ordered further preparations for the expected invasion, with the Luftwaffe tasked with attacking coastal defences, key communication targets, naval installations and concentrations of troops. Giving the Luftwaffe so many different targets was unhelpful: it led to uncoordinated, piecemeal attacks which resulted in little effective damage and relatively few casualties. This initial phase of the battle was ultimately a messy attempt to push Britain towards peace negotiations. It was not until 1 August that a further directive was issued by Hitler, this time identifying the RAF as the key, specific target in order to achieve aerial supremacy. He ordered a coordinated assault through attacks on Fighter Command aircraft, the whole air force structure and its supporting industries. This knock-out blow was scheduled to begin on or shortly after 5 August.

The Luftwaffe themselves were now much clearer about what was required. The senior commanders, including Kesselring and Sperrle, met with Göring on 6 August at the commander-in-chief's impressive Carinhall estate, located outside Berlin in the Schorfheide Forest. Their discussions led to the adoption of a straightforward and confident plan: the elimination of Fighter Command in the skies over southern England within four days. This victory would then be followed by an advance further up the country, targeting military and economic locations, until the Luftwaffe achieved full air superiority and could mount daylight attacks across the whole of Britain. Then it would be only a matter of time before British resolve would collapse, leading to either surrender or invasion. The opening day for the attack was codenamed Adlertag ('Day of the Eagles'). A spell of fine weather was required for optimum success, however, and so the attack was delayed repeatedly until a final date was chosen: 13 August 1940.

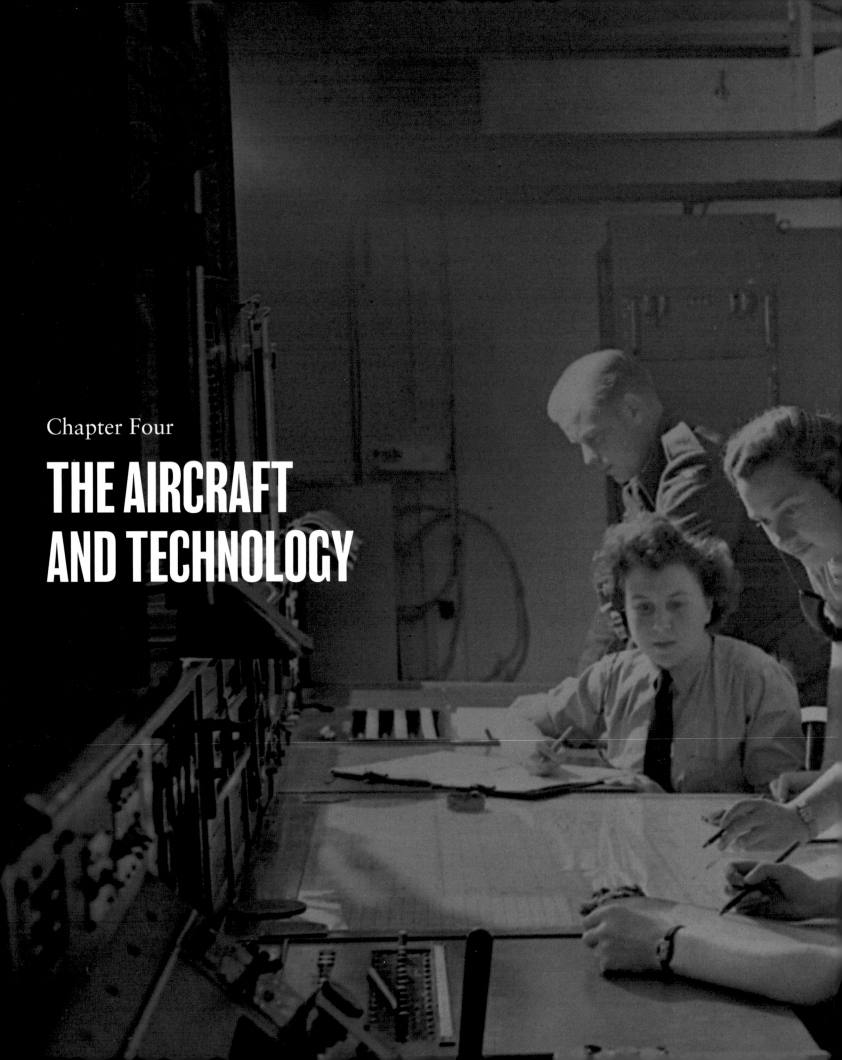

Chapter Four

THE AIRCRAFT
AND TECHNOLOGY

One distinctive aspect of the Battle of Britain is its strong association with the aircraft through which it was fought. No other individual conflict is so strongly linked to technology, with the Battle of Britain serving to highlight the advances made in a number of different areas by both sides. It could be argued that the aircraft available to fight the battle were among the best single-engine fighter aircraft in the world at that point.

On the British side, this meant mainly the Hawker Hurricane and the Supermarine Spitfire. While the Spitfire has perhaps become the aircraft most associated with the battle, the bulk of Fighter Command squadrons were usually made up of Hurricanes. This was because the Spitfire only became available in sufficient quantities during the late spring of 1940, and as a consequence their production lagged substantially behind the Hurricane until early the following year, once the Battle of Britain was over. Indeed, 11 Group had twice as many Hurricane squadrons in operation as Spitfire squadrons throughout the period of the battle.

But the Spitfire proved to be the most iconic aircraft of the battle. One might presume that the almost legendary reputation assigned to it only developed in the period since the war, yet the new aircraft was greatly admired at the time, with a clear fascination existing for its cutting-edge technology. The aircraft's speed, high performance and attractive elliptical wing design proved popular with pilots, while its association with the Battle of Britain meant that it would come to be seen as the aircraft synonymous with the British war effort and, in the longer term, part of the wider illustrative 'shorthand' for representing the Second World War. Interestingly, the new fighter was even admired by its opponents. Pilot Officer James Goodson, an American flying with No. 43 Squadron RAF, recalled an amusing encounter related to him by a colleague.

> When Peter Townsend went to see one of the German pilots that he'd shot down close to the base, the German said to him, 'I'm very glad to meet the Spitfire pilot who shot me down.' And Peter said, 'No, no, I was flying a Hurricane, I'm a Hurricane pilot.' And the German said, 'Would you do me a favour? If you are talking to any other Luftwaffe pilots, please tell them that I was shot down by a Spitfire.'

Of course some pilots preferred to stick with what they knew and were comfortable flying, and so favoured the Hurricane over the new competitor. Good-natured arguments over whether the Spitfire or Hurricane was the best British fighter were common, especially among the pilots themselves, as Geoffrey Page recalled.

> I was lucky because I had the unique experience of being one of the very few pilots during the Battle of Britain who had flown both

KEY AIRCRAFT

Supermarine Spitfire

First entering service in August 1938 at RAF Duxford in Cambridgeshire, the Spitfire was the iconic aircraft of the Battle of Britain and became the symbol of British defiance in the air. Designed by R J Mitchell, Supermarine's chief designer, it had an advanced all-metal airframe which made the aircraft both light and strong. Despite being less sturdy overall than some of its competitors, the Spitfire was faster than any other British fighter and had a responsiveness which impressed all the pilots who flew it. Crucially, it proved to be more than a match for the Luftwaffe's Messerschmitt Bf 109 and proved superior when flown at lower altitudes. Production was slow at first due to the aircraft being much more complicated to construct than the Hurricane, but between 1 June and 1 November 1940 some 724 Spitfires were built. By September 1940 Spitfires were in service with 18 different RAF squadrons.

(Above) A Spitfire of No. 19 Squadron RAF about to take off from Fowlmere, Cambridgeshire, in September 1940.

(Pages 96–97) Flight Officer P M Wright supervises as Sergeant K F Sperrin and WAAF operators Joan Lancaster, Elaine Miley, Gwen Arnold and Joyce Hollyoak work on the plotting map in the Receiver Room at Bawdsey Chain Home station, Suffolk. Taken in May 1945.

The construction of Merlin aircraft engines 'somewhere in England' in 1942. Female workers attach the induction manifolds to the cylinder blocks, before the blocks are fitted to the engine.

Hawker Hurricane

The Hurricane was the most common RAF Fighter Command aircraft during the Battle of Britain, used by 33 squadrons by September 1940. Some 1,367 were constructed between 1 June and 1 November 1940 – almost twice as many as the Spitfire. Its traditional design of a wood and metal framework covered in fabric was derived from earlier biplane fighters, and as such it was considered somewhat outdated despite later improvements. However, it remained a stable and rugged aircraft which could be maintained and repaired more easily than the newer and more complicated Spitfire. The limitations of the Hurricane meant that where possible Hurricane squadrons were directed against enemy bombers, while the superior and more manoeuvrable Spitfires targeted the fighter escorts. Despite its shortcomings, the Hurricane served successfully as the workhorse of Fighter Command and shot down some 656 German aircraft during the Battle of Britain.

(Above) Hurricane Mk Is of No. 245 Squadron RAF, in flight from Aldergrove, near Belfast, in November 1940.

(Left) A rear-gunner's-eye view of three Spitfires from No. 610 Squadron RAF 'attacking' a Blenheim as part of a training operation, 24 July 1940.

the Hurricane and the Spitfire. They were both lovable, but in their different ways – they were delightful airplanes. I tend to give an example of the bulldog and the greyhound, the Hurricane being the bulldog and the greyhound being the Spitfire. One's a sort of tough working animal and the other one's a sleek, fast dog. But I think their characteristics were comparable to the dog world. If anything the Hurricane was slightly easier. It wasn't as fast and didn't have the rate of climb. But during the actual Battle of Britain itself, what really evolved was that the Hurricanes would attack the German bomber formations and the Spitfires, because of their extra capability of climbing, they would go up and attack the German fighter escorts. But in the earlier stages I found that we were getting involved with both bombers and fighters when we were flying Hurricanes.

Perhaps the fairest summation of the aircrafts' respective strengths was offered by test pilot Jeffrey Quill, who had considerable experience flying both.

> I took the view myself that it took both planes to win the Battle of Britain. Neither would have succeeded on its own because the Hurricanes required the Spitfire squadrons to attack the Messerschmitt 109s while the Hurricanes concentrated on destroying the bombers. They were both there together and they both depended on each other. You sometimes hear people saying, 'The Spitfire won the Battle of Britain.' Well, that's absolute rubbish. The Spitfire and the Hurricane won the Battle of Britain.

Despite the respective strengths of the British fighters, the Luftwaffe flew what was arguably the world's best all-round fighter aircraft, the Messerschmitt Bf 109. Heavily armed, it boasted a DB 601 engine with a hydraulic supercharger, which enabled the aircraft to fight more robustly at high altitudes above 20,000 feet. Since height was a distinct advantage in any aerial dogfight, this gave the Me 109 an essential edge despite the fact that it could be out-turned by both the Hurricane and Spitfire. German pilots, including Major Hans-Ekkehard Bob, praised the efficiency of the aircraft and developed special flying tactics as they got to know its particular characteristics.

> The Me-109 had in case of motor failure a gliding angle of 1:13, for example of a height of 1 km you could in the best possible way cover a distance of 13 km. One day I was shot at over England, approximately 80 km from the French coast, at a height of 4,000 meters in such a way that the cooling system of the motor failed. Usually we had to put the air screw to gliding position and try to glide, as mentioned 1:13 homeward. According to my consideration this was normally not possible from a height of 4,000 meters. Therefore I let the motor, being in neutral gear, become cooler first. When the temperature had fallen to normal, I switched the ignition on again, opened the throttle and went up as high as possible until

KEY AIRCRAFT

Boulton Paul Defiant

The Defiant was a British two-seater fighter with a four-gun power-operated turret. The aircraft had no forward firing capability, having to rely on its turret to shoot down enemies while they were located either above or behind; once the Luftwaffe became aware of this quirk of design, any initial advantage of surprise was reversed. The Defiant was intended primarily as a bomber interceptor, but the weight caused by the turret and extra crew member meant that it was much slower and less manoeuvrable than the speedy fighters it usually opposed. Despite early battles over Dunkirk in which Defiants had proven very vulnerable to conventional enemy fighters, Fighter Command rashly sent its two Defiant squadrons into action in July and August 1940, which resulted in separate massacres at the hands of the Luftwaffe. As a consequence, the aircraft was withdrawn from daylight service and converted to the less-demanding night fighter role. The Defiant therefore played a relatively minor role in the Battle of Britain.

(Above) A formation of Boulton Paul Defiants of No. 264 Squadron RAF in flight, August 1940.

(Left) A CH (Chain Home) Radar Station on the East Coast by William Thomas Rawlinson, 1946.

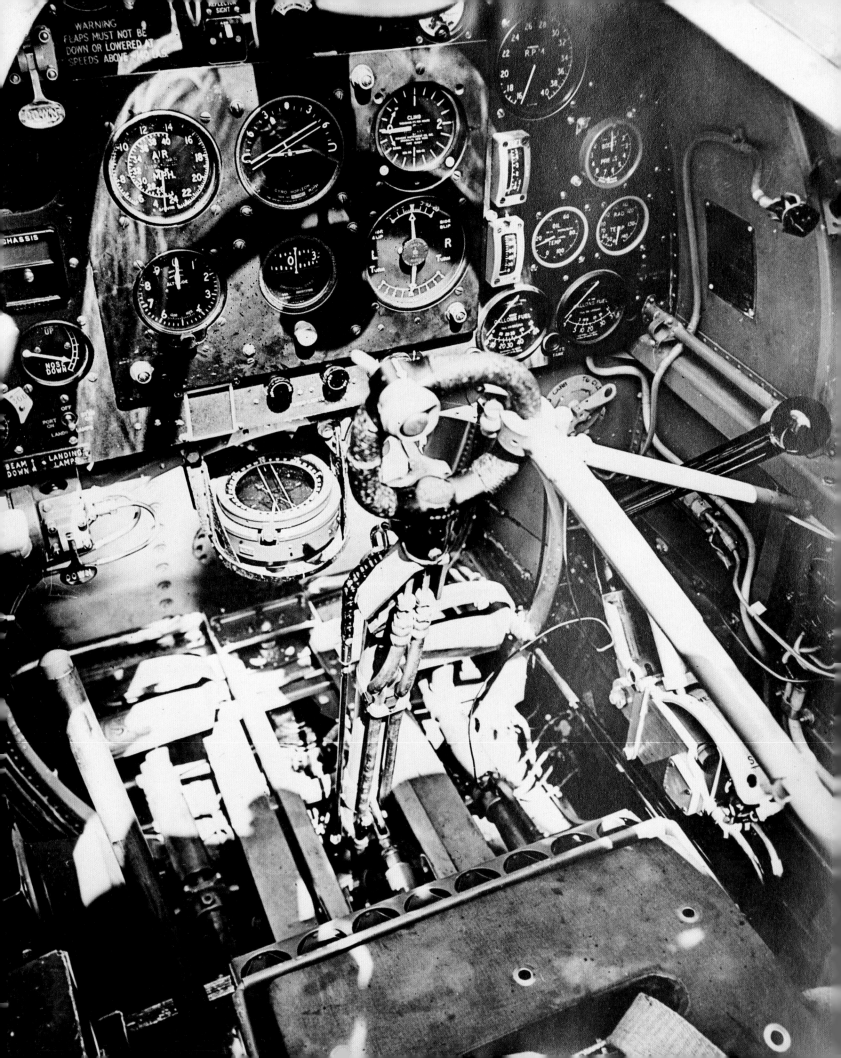

the motor was overheated again; I repeated this for several times and barely reached the French coast where I made a forced landing on the sand beach. According to my experience report this method was later on called 'to Bob' across the Channel.

One of the greatest limiting factors for aircraft was the range in which they could operate, determined by their fuel load and home airfield. The Nazi occupation of France and Norway improved Germany's prospects for an invasion of Britain by greatly increasing the range of their aircraft. Flying from bases in northern France, the Me 109 fighter could now reach as far as London, although using up fuel during combat greatly reduced their range. Pilots needed to be aware of their fuel levels and location in order to make sure that enough fuel remained in reserve to reach home. Such limitations meant that the Luftwaffe could therefore only really challenge air superiority across an arc stretching over the south-east of Britain, across Kent, Sussex and Surrey.

In terms of the other technology available to either side, Britain had perhaps the biggest advantage. The country benefitted from a complex system of observation, providing advanced warning of any incoming enemy attack, which successfully countered the element of surprise enjoyed by the Germans. Often referred to as the 'Dowding System', after Fighter Command's commander-in-chief, the network brought together ground defences, fighter aircraft and specialised technology in a unified system of defence. Central to the system was a clearly defined chain of command, allowing both intelligence about incoming raids and the communication of orders to flow smoothly to appropriate units. It was not just the fighter aircraft which benefitted from such a system but also the other elements of Britain's defence network such as anti-aircraft batteries, searchlights and barrage balloons. By contrast, the Germans lacked this very significant advantage: they had no way of tracking where their enemy was and no way of controlling their overall fighter force during an active mission.

The central hub of the Dowding System was Fighter Command's headquarters at Bentley Priory in Stanmore, on the outskirts of London. There, intelligence reports were received from stations situated all along the coast of southern and eastern England as they detected approaching aircraft. This information was plotted out on a large map table, then relayed in turn to the headquarters of each Fighter Command Group and the individual sector stations at each airfield. Every sector station was equipped with its own operations room, from which fighters could be directed into combat. Once a sector station had been activated by its group commander, the local commanders would decide which of their squadrons should be launched. The aircraft were then directed to their targets through the use of radio-telephony direction-finding (R/T-D/F), commonly abbreviated as RDF.

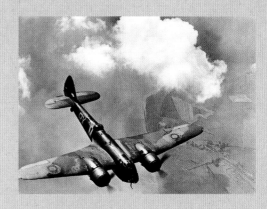

KEY AIRCRAFT

Bristol Blenheim

The Blenheim was a twin-engined aircraft which was designed to be a light bomber, but it also saw some use as a British fighter during the Battle of Britain. In service since 1937, it was one of the first aircraft built with an all-metal, stressed skin and boasted retractable landing gear, flaps and a powered gun turret. While effective enough as a fast light bomber, the Blenheim soon compared unfavourably to the newer designs of single-engine fighter aircraft and became outclassed for daylight use. It continued as a night fighter, along with the Bristol Beaufighter from September 1940, with both aircraft proving more successful in this alternative role. The Blenheim was also the most common aircraft flown by Bomber Command for its anti-invasion missions against German shipping located around the French ports.

(Above) Blenheim of No. 25 Squadron RAF in flight, likely photographed in 1939.

(Left) An instructional photograph showing the instrument panel and flying controls of a Spitfire.

(Pages 106–107) An aerial photograph of the Fighter Command headquarters at RAF Bentley Priory, located in Stanmore, Middlesex.

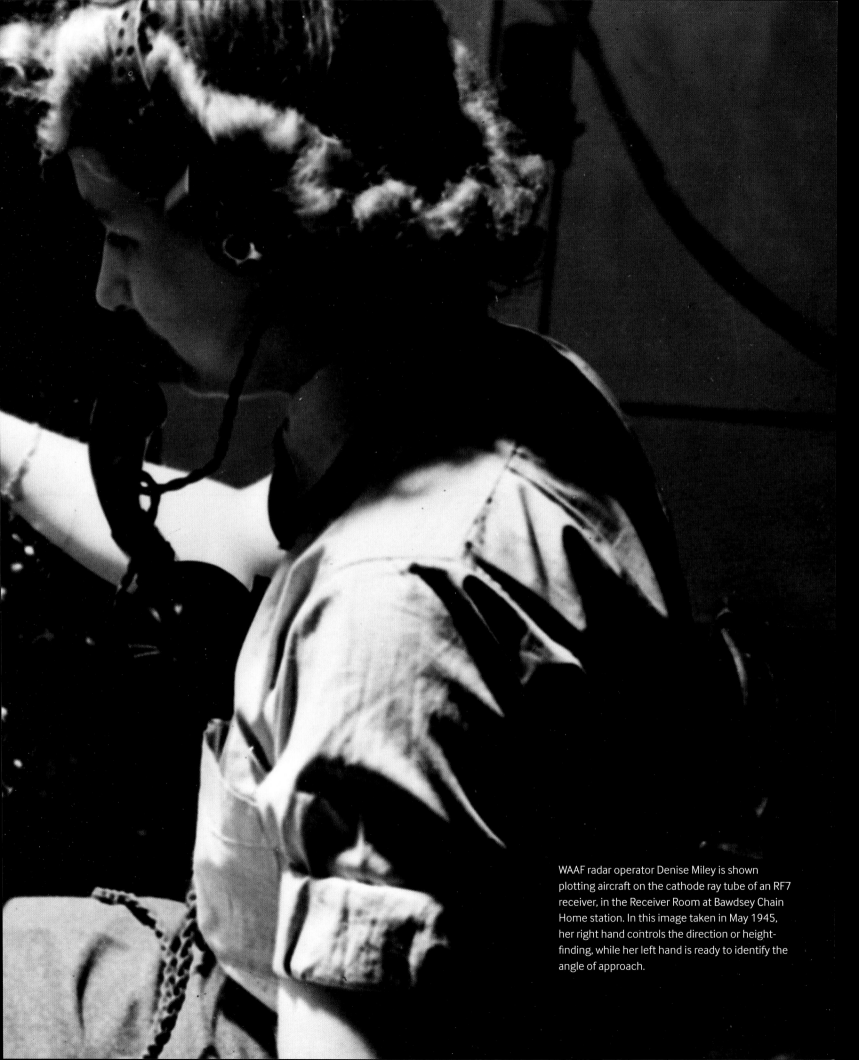

WAAF radar operator Denise Miley is shown plotting aircraft on the cathode ray tube of an RF7 receiver, in the Receiver Room at Bawdsey Chain Home station. In this image taken in May 1945, her right hand controls the direction or height-finding, while her left hand is ready to identify the angle of approach.

RDF technology really formed the heart of this early-warning system and was an early version of what is now known as radar (radio detection and ranging). It was based on the discovery that short-wave radio pulses were reflected by aircraft and could be visualised on a screen by using a cathode ray tube. The system was first deployed in Britain in 1935 and by the time of the Battle of Britain it was still undergoing continual development and improvement. Given the codename 'Chain Home' (CH), a series of stations was constructed all along the southern and eastern coastline of Britain which could detect the height and range of approaching aircraft up to 200 miles distant. A second 'Chain Home Low' (CHL) system of substations was also operated to detect incoming aircraft or shipping at a much lower height and within an operating range of 30 miles.

Harry Harris had initially been called up to serve with a searchlight unit based at Southampton on the south coast, but in the summer of 1940 he was posted to the nearby Hayling Island for training in the new RDF technology.

> On this first day we were told that we were about to be introduced to the most secret weapon that Britain possessed and it was made very clear to us that the penalty for breathing one word about the things we were to learn would have only one result, we would be shot. CHL stations were situated on the South Coast [and] were the first Radar stations... Actually they gave very little information other than the general direction and range of approaching enemy formations. Like all Radar sets, CHL stations could identify friendly and enemy formations by a device carried in all friendly aircraft called IFF (Identification, Friend or Foe). This was a small radio transmitter on the same wavelength as the Radar which caused the signal from a friendly aircraft on the cathode ray tube to flicker at regular intervals. Pilots who forgot to switch on their IFF were very unpopular, as they always caused a full Air Raid alert.

The system required constant vigilance, and as raids increased in regularity, the personnel manning the Chain Home stations had to work long and stressful hours.

> At this time, the end of 1940... we were in action for twenty out of each twenty four hours, and it was at that time I discovered a person could make do with an average of four hours sleep a day. The man operating the transmitter could catnap even when we were in action but the rest of the team on duty had to be completely alert all the time.

The Chain Home system was certainly not infallible, as height readings could be significantly out and the time spent between sighting an enemy and scrambling fighters to meet them might be far too long to provide effective opposition to a raid. A German aircraft could cross the

KEY AIRCRAFT
Messerschmitt Bf 109

The Luftwaffe could legitimately boast that with the Bf 109 they flew what was arguably the best fighter aircraft in the world in 1940. It proved to be faster than the Spitfire at higher altitude, could dive more rapidly and carried a more effective armament of two cannons and two machine guns. Most Bf 109 pilots had a greater degree of combat experience than their RAF counterparts, at least during the initial stages of the Battle of Britain, which also conferred a major advantage. However, the Messerschmitt did not have the range to fly further than London and carried only seven seconds' worth of cannon ammunition, which was an obvious limitation to its operational usefulness. There were around 1,100 Bf 109s and 1,126 operational pilots available at the beginning of the battle, yet an enormous 650 of these aircraft would ultimately be shot down.

(Above) A Messerschmitt Bf 109, ready for take-off.

The Chain Home installation at Poling, West Sussex, photographed in 1945. On the left are three (originally four) in-line 360-foot (110-metre) steel towers, between which the transmitter aerials are slung, with the heavily protected transmitter building in front. On the right are four 240-foot (73-metre) wooden receiver towers, with the receiver building in the middle.

The interior of the Sector 'G' Operations Room at Duxford, Cambridgeshire, in September 1940. The call signs of fighter squadrons controlled by this sector can be seen on the wall behind the operator, who sits third from the left. The fighter controller is sitting fifth from the left, and on the extreme right, behind the army liaison officer, are the wireless operators who are in direct contact with the aircraft.

An anti-aircraft searchlight and crew located at the Royal Hospital at Chelsea in London, 17 April 1940.

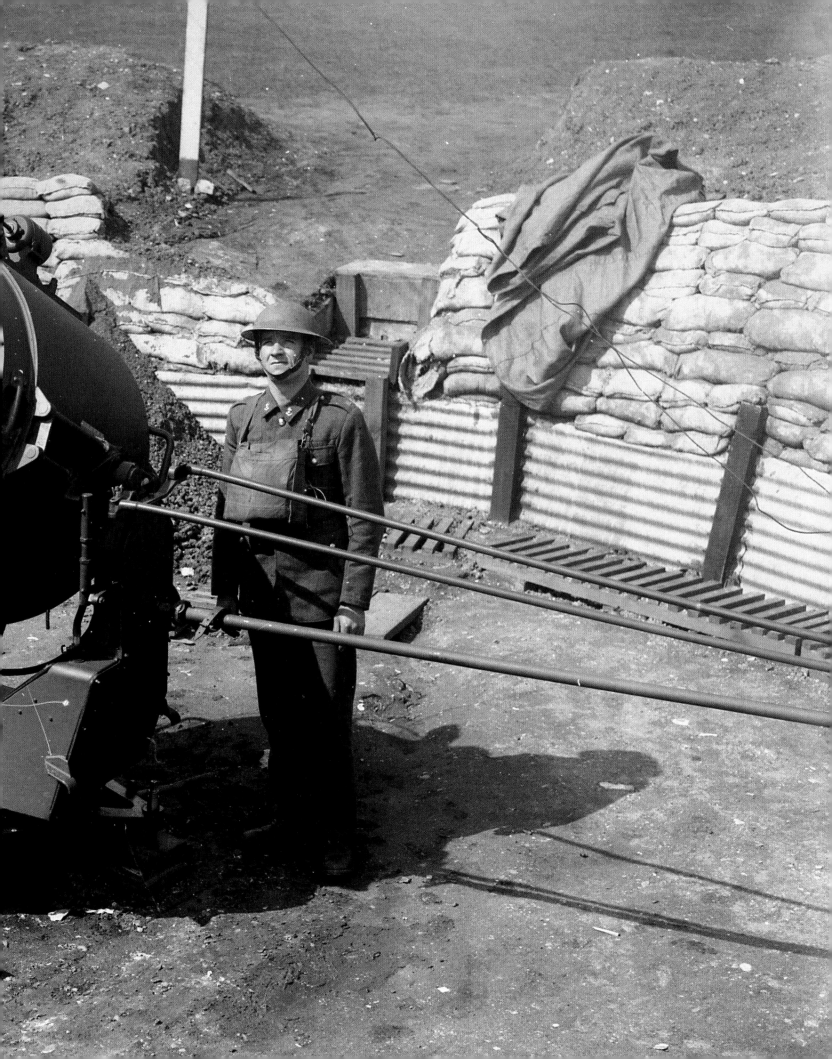

A member of the Observer Corps listens for
the approach of aircraft while his colleague
sleeps, 29 February 1940.

Three members of the Observer Corps chart
the movements of aircraft in their sector with
a plotting instrument, summer 1940.

Channel in around six minutes, yet it would take at least four minutes to scramble fighters to intercept it. RDF was also of little use once aircraft were inland, and therefore as soon as the enemy had crossed the coast and could be seen with the naked eye, the RDF system of advance warning would be supplemented by the Observer Corps.

The origins of the Observer Corps lay in the Raid Reporting System set up in 1925. This was one of several organisations created as part of Britain's general push towards preparing its civilian population for the likelihood of enemy bombing. By the outbreak of war there were around 1,000 observation posts manned by 30,000 observers, each trained in aircraft recognition and ways of estimating both height and distance. The information they collected was relayed to Observer Corps centres and subsequently to the group headquarters and sector stations, where it would contribute to the existing intelligence being amassed. The system worked fine in good weather, but badly in cloud and rain; as a result, a lot of unreliable information was often submitted, which failed to add much value.

Further advantages to be gained from new technology were identified by RAF wireless interception stations. Their operators listened in to the low-level radio traffic of German aircrews, from which they were often able to collect accurate reports on the origin, destination and range of the enemy aircraft. This intelligence was relayed to the appropriate RAF squadrons and passed to the Allied pilots in the air. Rosemary Horstmann was serving with the Women's Auxiliary Air Force at RAF Hawkinge, near Folkestone in Kent. As part of the Y Service, she had the job of listening in to the German pilots' wireless transmissions.

> It was very dramatic because several of the girls working with us had boyfriends who were pilots and so they would find themselves in the situation of monitoring a battle in which their fiancés were fighting. We were writing down what the German pilots were saying and they were saying things like, 'I've got him', 'He's gone down', and you would hear people screaming.

While the Dowding System relied largely on the aircraft of Fighter Command as its main weapon of defence, this was heavily supplemented by ground-based elements such as anti-aircraft guns, searchlights and barrage balloons. Many hundreds of gun emplacements were established across the south and east of England, especially around London and along the coast, ready to target incoming aircraft. J W Clark was serving with an anti-aircraft unit at Dover, and he described in his diary how the early-warning system was implemented for their guns. Gun batteries were fully integrated with Fighter Command and activated from their headquarters, in line with the overall Dowding System.

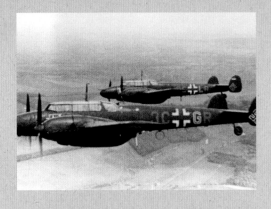

KEY AIRCRAFT
Messerschmitt Bf 110

The two-seater Bf 110 was designed to function as a long-range heavy escort fighter or Zerstörer ('Destroyer'). It was much faster than the Hurricane, comparable in speed to the Spitfire, and was well armed and extremely effective in terms of bombing accuracy. But the Bf 110 lacked manoeuvrability and was markedly inferior to the more nimble RAF fighters, becoming a liability when attempting to guard the larger bomber formations. After numerous losses, the Luftwaffe was forced to use Bf 109s to escort the Bf 110s. However, the aircraft still proved very effective when used for low-level attacks against factories and airfields, although the Germans failed to see this potential as a fighter bomber and only one Luftwaffe unit was trained for such a role.

(Above) A flight of Messerschmitt Bf 110s.

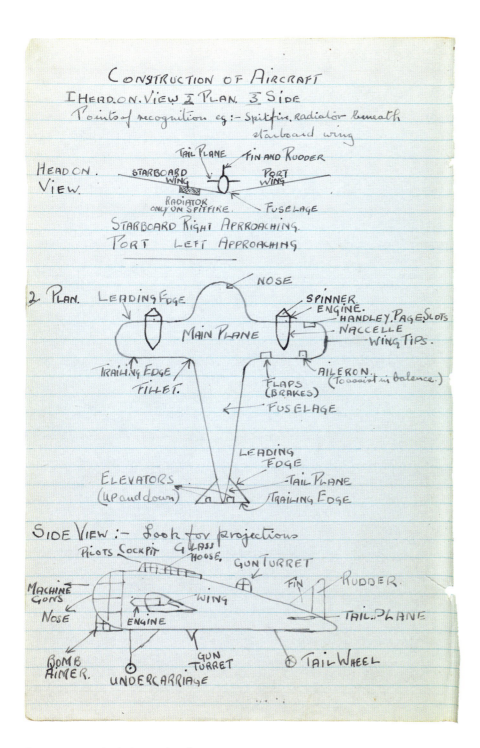

Some notes made during an aircraft
observation course, illustrating the key
elements of an aircraft to look for in order
to make an accurate identification.

KEY AIRCRAFT

Heinkel He 111

The He 111 was the most important of the
Luftwaffe's early bombers and was used in
greater numbers for this role than any other
type of aircraft during the Battle of Britain.
The aircraft was well known because its wing
shape gave it a distinctive silhouette. But in
many ways it could have been considered
as obsolete in 1940, since its bomb load of
2,000 kilograms was insufficient for modern
strategic bombing and its slow speed
and poor armament did not help. Various
measures were introduced to increase the
aircraft's defensive capability, yet these
proved largely ineffective and the Heinkel,
like other German bomber types, remained
extremely vulnerable to attack by fast RAF
fighters. It was a powerful aircraft in terms
of its structural strength, however, which
was shown to withstand considerable
punishment.

(*Above*) Luftwaffe Heinkel He 111 bombers
flying in formation.

By July 1941, when this photograph was taken, the shortage of men meant that far more women were assigned to the RAF's Balloon Command and many formed all-women WAAF crews.

(Right) Kite barrage balloons and their attendant winches are walked out of No. 1 Airship Shed at Cardington, Bedfordshire, for handling practice by No. 1 Balloon Training Unit. October 1940.

In the command post dugout, there was a large scale map of the area, and with our particular gun site prominently marked. The map was squared, and each square numbered. There were also two circles, with our gun site in the centre, the outer one representing a radius of 30 miles, and the inner, 20 miles.

Information was received at a central control room at Dover, called the GOR [Gun Operations Room]. It came from the Observer Corps, the RAF, other gun sites and most important of all, radio-location, when any aircraft were flying, even as far away as the Essex coast, and some thirty miles out into the North Sea as well as those close to us. This information, consisting of the number of the map square, the number of aircraft in the formation, their height and speed, the direction in which they were flying, and whether hostile, friendly, or unidentified, was broadcast to all gun sites. All this was duly noted, and a mark made in the appropriate map square. Then a minute or two later would come more information, showing that the aircraft concerned had moved into an adjacent square, and perhaps changed directions or height. Another mark was made on the map, and a constant stream of messages from G.O.R. kept us up to date with all movements.

Each mark on the map was called a 'plot', and the successive plots were joined by a continuous pencil line, so that the course and latest position, etc. were visible at a glance. The aircraft whose movements we were plotting were always referred to as 'raids'... When hostile or unidentified raids came into our 30 mile radius we received from G.O.R. an 'alert', but sometimes this was given for even more distant raids. An alert meant that we must be prepared to man the guns, etc. at a moment's notice, and if it was night everyone was awakened and told to be ready. If the raid came into the 20 mile radius, the 'alarm' was given and every man jumped to his action station and a sharp look out [was] kept in the direction from whence the raid was expected.

Closely linked to anti-aircraft defences were searchlights, heavy-duty machines capable of sending strong shafts of light skywards in order to illuminate enemy aircraft and serve as a guide for the guns. Harry Harris served in a searchlight unit based at Southampton.

ELSIE (Search Light Control) was used to control a few of the larger searchlights, the 150 cm type, which were able to fasten on to individual enemy bombers and were then joined by the smaller, 90 cm lights in the vicinity. Once a plane had been caught in three beams, it had very little chance of escaping as, whichever way it turned, it was always turning towards one of the lights. Of course, as it got out of range of one light, it came into the range of fresh lights.

KEY AIRCRAFT

Dornier Do 17

The Dornier Do 17, with its twin tail and 'shoulder wing', was designed to outrun other aircraft and it remained speedy at low altitude, making it popular with its crews because it was harder to hit than other German bombers. The aircraft was based on a pre-war design for a high-speed mail plane, but was converted into a bomber by the Nazi air ministry. It saw service during the Spanish Civil War, and by the beginning of the Second World War it was, alongside the Heinkel He 111, one of the main German bombers. But by the time that three Luftwaffe bomber wings were equipped with Do 17s at the height of the Battle of Britain, the aircraft was already virtually out of date. Despite working well at low altitude, it could only carry 1,000 kilograms of bombs and had a limited range. In a similar story to the Heinkel, its defences were weak and severe losses followed, not least on 18 August when eight Dorniers were shot down and nine damaged in attacks to the south of London. This led to production of Do 17s being terminated in the summer of 1940.

(*Above*) A Dornier Do 17 preparing to take off from an airfield, February 1941.

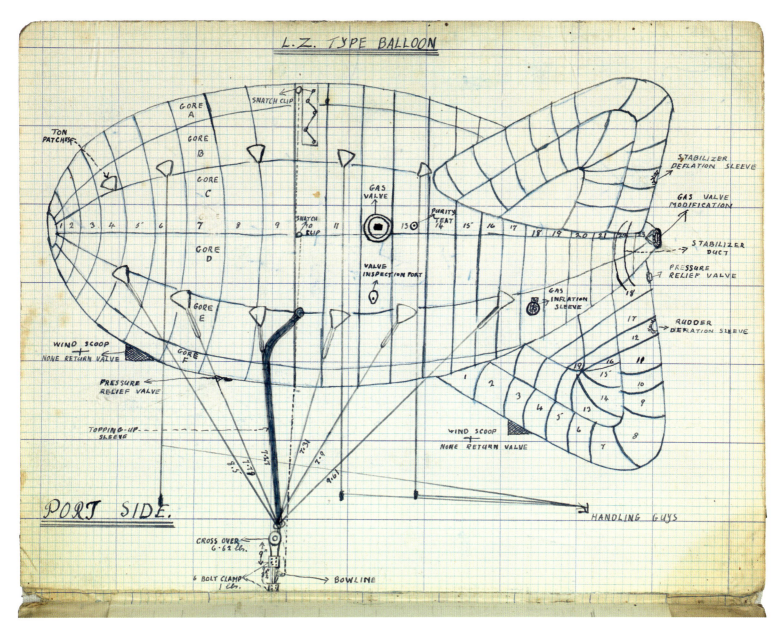

This illustration of a barrage balloon was drawn during a training course undertaken by a balloon team based in Sheffield, 1940.

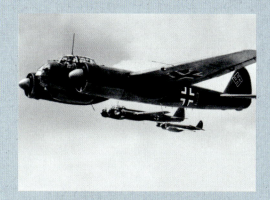

KEY AIRCRAFT
Junkers Ju 88

The Junkers Ju 88 was the most modern of Germany's medium bombers, first introduced to operational service in 1939 and designed to outrun any attacking fighters. However, the promising new design was compromised by Colonel Ernst Udet, the Luftwaffe's head of procurement, who demanded that the aircraft be capable of dive-bombing. The structural changes which were necessary for this role increased the aircraft's weight, in turn reducing its performance and also serving to delay production. It proved just as vulnerable to RAF fighters as other German bombers during the Battle of Britain, but later matured into one of the most versatile and important of the Luftwaffe's aircraft, ultimately serving as a bomber, night fighter, reconnaissance aircraft, heavy fighter and even (in heavily modified form) flying bomb.

(Above) A formation of Junkers Ju 88A-1s, the original bomber version of the highly adaptable Junkers Ju 88 aircraft.

(Left) A firefighting unit ready for action at Duxford, Cambridgeshire, during September/October 1940. One airman is wearing a fire-resistant asbestos suit for rescue work.

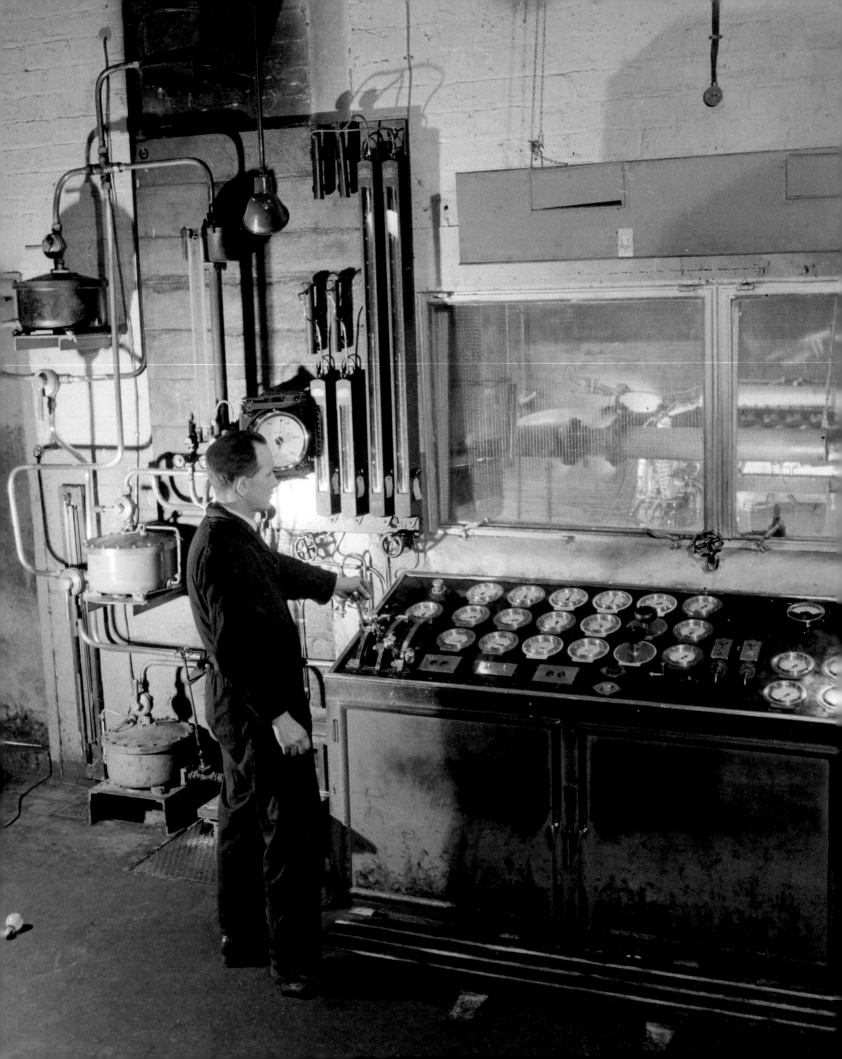

While Britain had spent considerable time and effort in preparing for its defence throughout the pre-war period, there were still far fewer anti-aircraft guns than had originally been planned for. By June 1940 there were only 1,204 heavy and 581 light anti-aircraft guns to cover the entire country, leading planners to distribute the weapons more heavily within the sectors which needed them most, across the south and east. The entire country was split up into 130 warning districts, and when enemy aircraft were identified as approaching from 20 miles distant, a yellow warning was activated, which placed the emergency services on alert. Five minutes later a red warning followed, which triggered air raid sirens and an anti-aircraft barrage. A green warning indicated that the threat had passed.

Working in tandem with the artillery units was RAF Balloon Command, whose task was to operate the giant tethered barrage balloons that floated above the potential targets of German bombers. The balloons forced the Luftwaffe to operate at higher altitudes, reducing the accuracy of bombing and bringing them into the range of anti-aircraft guns. Members of Balloon Command had to raise or lower the balloons to the correct height using winches. They were also responsible for keeping the balloons inflated and in position, which could be very difficult, particularly in bad weather and during high winds. While serving as an effective deterrent to low-flying aircraft, barrage balloons were sometimes used as target practice by particularly plucky Luftwaffe pilots who perhaps saw them as an irresistible challenge, despite the attention of Britain's defences, as gunner J W Clark recalled on 29 August.

> A 109 pilot had a good time. He made a surprise swoop on a balloon and got it, then turned and got another. Still not content, he made yet another turn and this time got two more, making four in all. He certainly had guts to go through the barrage three times, especially when the Bofors gunners were fully awake and after his blood.

The overall systems of defence would prove invaluable to the British war effort during the Battle of Britain, especially as the German strategy developed and began to move towards specific ground targets. The war in the air was to spread to a wider form of attack.

KEY AIRCRAFT

Junkers Ju 87 Stuka

The infamous Ju 87 Stuka became chiefly known for playing such a vital part in the successful German Blitzkrieg attacks at the beginning of the war. Its name was an abbreviated form of the German term for dive-bomber ('Sturzkampfflugzeug'). The Ju 87 was first used in combat in Spain during 1937, and it became a strong propaganda image illustrating advanced German air power. The aircraft was easily recognised by its gull wing design, and siren mechanisms mounted on the aircraft's landing gear created a screeching noise when delivering bombing attacks with great accuracy in a near-vertical dive. But while proving highly effective during the campaigns in Poland and France, where Germany enjoyed air superiority, it was a different case in the skies over Britain. Despite some initial successes, the Stukas suffered significant losses due to RAF fighters, and on 18 August alone, 12 Ju 87s were shot down and many others damaged or written off in crashes. Such losses meant that the Stuka was gradually withdrawn from the battle.

(*Above*) A Junkers Ju 87 Stuka in flight.

(*Left*) An engineer stands at his control panel in the test bed of this Merlin aircraft engine factory in 1942. Visible through the window is an engine which is undergoing testing.

WAAF plotters at work in the Operations Room at No. 11 Group headquarters in Uxbridge, Middlesex during 1942. Plotters worked in three shifts in teams of about ten, tracking the size and direction of incoming German raids using wooden blocks displayed around a large table. These blocks showed the name of the raid and an estimate of its strength, and arrows placed behind each block showed the raid's direction. The arrows were colour-coded to indicate how up-to-date the information was. Friendly aircraft were plotted in a separate room.

Chapter Five

THE TARGETING OF AIRFIELDS, AUGUST 1940

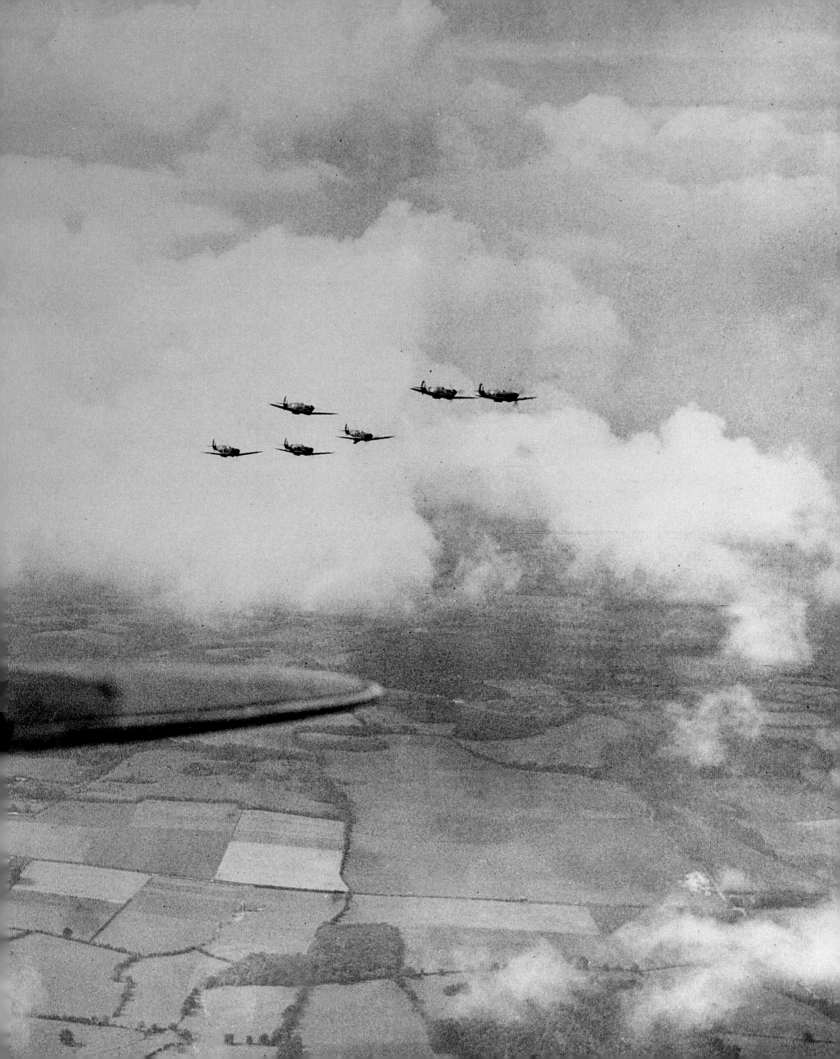

Göring's new strategy of 6 August 1940 shifted the emphasis of the Luftwaffe's aerial campaign much more clearly onto one, straightforward aim: to destroy the RAF's Fighter Command. The Luftwaffe intended to launch their initial strike, Adlertag (Day of the Eagles), almost immediately, but kept delaying while waiting for the most opportune weather conditions. They finally chose the morning of Tuesday, 13 August, but even then they delayed the initial assault until that afternoon. News of this postponement failed to reach a number of airfields in sufficient time, however, to prevent hundreds of aircraft taking off towards the British coast. This incomplete, part-strength force meant that the opening of the Battle of Britain proper (as far as the Germans were concerned) began with a whimper rather than a bang.

Indeed, although the Luftwaffe were clear that their concerted effort to eliminate Fighter Command was really only now beginning with a vengeance, the British completely failed to recognise the initiative and felt that the 13 August raid was simply a continuation of the existing bombing campaign. In fact, some perceived intensification of German bombing earlier that month had prompted the Air Ministry to regard 8 August as the beginning of the battle proper, although many disagreed with this decision, including Lord Dowding. Keith Park only noticed a particular change on 18 August, when attacks began to intensify and move further inland, leading to fighter airfields being targeted more frequently. Ceaseless attacks would now be made by the Luftwaffe on British airfields by both day and night, in preparation for a German invasion which was scheduled for 15 September. The Battle of Britain had now most definitely begun.

*

Between 12 August and 6 September, the Luftwaffe made 53 major attacks on British airfields, of which 32 were specific Fighter Command stations. All but two of these attacks were against locations within 11 Group's area, around London and the south-east. As many as 1,000 raids were carried out in total over the country, equating to an average of around 35 per day, although most of these proved to be relatively small-scale attacks against industrial installations, communications targets and air force supply depots.

The single largest loss of life was suffered at Biggin Hill airfield in Kent, on the most southern outskirts of London, where on 30 August some 39 people were killed and 25 injured. Those airfields which suffered the worst were those within easy reach from the Luftwaffe airfields of France, near the Kent and Sussex coastlines. It was the Germans' aim to destroy as many aircraft on the ground as they could, as well as removing the airfield infrastructure which would facilitate their storage, repair and construction. Although 42 aircraft were destroyed on the ground from bombing raids during the first week of the attacks, the

(Pages 130–131) A distant view of Spitfires from No. 610 Squadron RAF, based at Biggin Hill, just outside London, 24 July 1940.

RAF quickly adopted very effective camouflage techniques to hide the targets as best they could. A system of dispersal was also introduced in order to make sure fewer large numbers of aircraft were in any one location at any time. Dispersing aircraft around the country also allowed damaged ones to be replaced at short notice, while air patrols served to protect those aircraft which were exposed on the ground while refuelling. Such actions meant that only 14 further British aircraft would be destroyed on the ground during this period.

But by the end of August, German intelligence sources estimated that at least eight British airfields had been completely destroyed while the rest were severely ineffective in terms of the damage they had sustained. They calculated that since Adlertag the RAF had lost half of its total fighter force, against the Germans' losses of only 12 per cent. In early September, Göring was told that Fighter Command had a mere hundred serviceable fighters left to sustain the battle. To him and the other Luftwaffe commanders, the Battle of Britain had been more or less won within just a few weeks.

But this was far from being the truth. On 1 September there were actually 701 operational aircraft in use by Fighter Command, and on 6 September this had risen to 738, with 256 extra planes newly built and ready for imminent despatch. RAF records show a cumulative loss of 444 aircraft during the month between 6 August and 2 September, all but 34 of which were Spitfires or Hurricanes from Fighter Command. By comparison, the Luftwaffe recorded 443 fighter losses – a statistic which was, coincidentally, almost identical. A very big gap therefore existed between the German commanders' perceptions of how the battle was going and the actual reality in the skies above Britain. While both sides had lost almost exactly the same number of fighter aircraft, both still had more than enough reserves to keep fighting the battle, despite the German perception that the British were already beaten.

In terms of operational pilot strength, too, the British were far from defeated. During August, however, the casualty rate within Fighter Command would rise to 22 per cent of the total pilot strength, which was a rate of loss higher than the new intake from operational training units. The solution to reduce this overall loss rate was to reinforce the squadrons of 11 Group, the worst-hit part of Fighter Command, by moving pilots to it from other fighter groups. This system was based on categorising squadrons in different ways. 'A' Squadrons were kept at a full strength of around twenty pilots, 'B' Squadrons were sustained near full strength but assigned to other key sectors, and 'C' Squadrons (each consisting of only five or six pilots) were set up in the 'safe' areas of 12 and 13 Groups in order to prepare the intake of trainees for eventual combat in the south-east. A rotation system within frontline squadrons gave pilots some respite too, although it did mean that those who were less experienced were thrown into combat much sooner than was ideal.

A Dornier Do 17Z-3 burns itself out after crash-landing at Prince's Golf Club on Sandwich Flats, near Ramsgate, following an attack on Hornchurch on 31 August 1940.

Two Hurricanes of No. 32 Squadron RAF come in
to land for refuelling and rearming at Biggin Hill,
just outside London, in August 1940.

Sergeant Joan Mortimer, Flight Officer Elspeth Henderson and Sergeant Helen Turner, recipients of the Military Medal for Gallantry, standing outside damaged buildings at Biggin Hill, near London, 1940. All three were WAAF teleprinter operators who stayed at their posts and continued to work the defence lines during the heavy Luftwaffe attacks on Biggin Hill on 1 September 1940.

Boulton Paul Defiants of No. 264 Squadron RAF
at Kirton in Lincolnshire, August 1940.

A film still taken from gun camera footage
of Luftwaffe Heinkel He 111 bombers under
attack, 1940.

Flight Lieutenant James Brindley Nicolson VC (shown in the centre, playing what looks like a flute) playing in a band while recovering in hospital, 1940. During an engagement with the enemy on 16 August 1940, Nicolson's Hurricane had been seriously damaged and set on fire, yet he remained in combat despite suffering serious wounds. He eventually baled out and parachuted to safety.

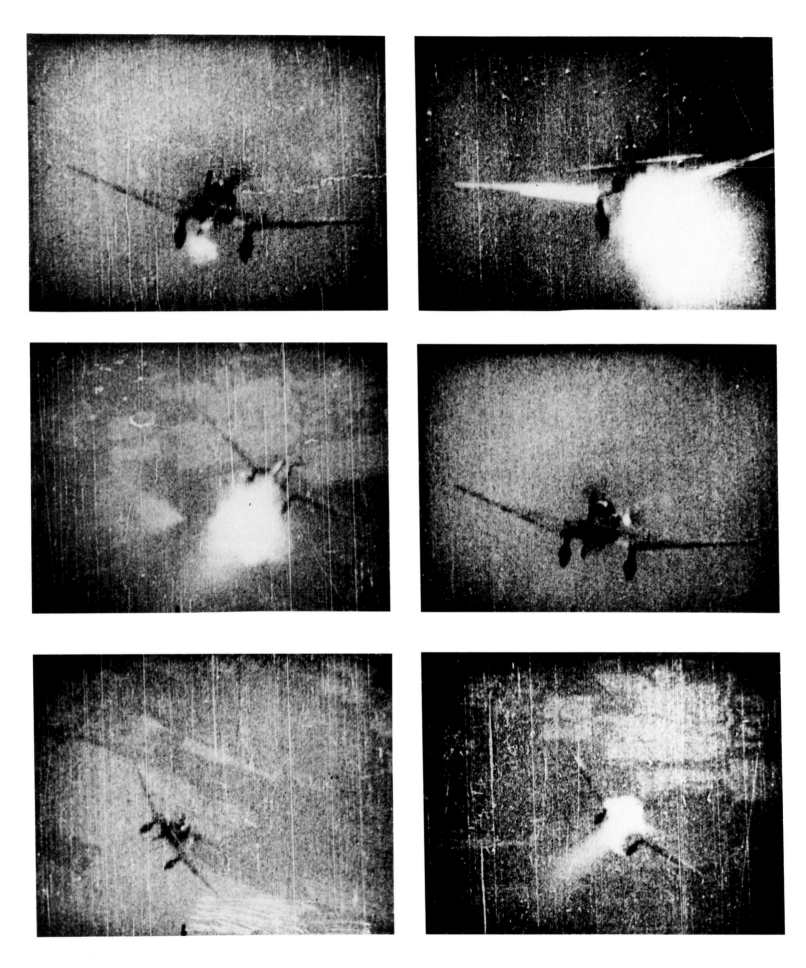

The Battle of Britain A Visual History

Airmen and civilians examine a shot-down Messerschmitt Bf 109E-4 in a wheat field on the south coast, 1940.

(Left) Frames from gun camera footage showing a Ju 87 Stuka being shot down by an RAF fighter, 1940.

When Churchill made his famous speech on 20 August in which he referred to 'The Few', it was within this context of regular attacks against the RAF's Fighter Command, whether against its airfields or clashes in the sky. But his quote has commonly been used slightly out of context. The Battle of Britain only featured briefly within his speech, with the prime minister instead focusing on the problems being experienced in fighting the Italians in North Africa. Nor did he single out fighter pilots alone for praise; he talked more about the important role of Bomber Command in attacking German targets in France and so working to prevent invasion.

> All hearts go out to the fighter pilots, whose brilliant actions we see with our own eyes day after day; but we must never forget that all the time, night after night, month after month, our bomber squadrons travel far into Germany, find their targets in the darkness by the highest navigational skill, aim their attacks, often under the heaviest fire, often with serious loss, with deliberate careful discrimination, and inflict shattering blows upon the whole of the technical and war-making structure of the Nazi power. On no part of the Royal Air Force does the weight of the war fall more heavily than on the daylight bombers who will play an invaluable part in the case of invasion and whose unflinching zeal it has been necessary in the meanwhile on numerous occasions to restrain.

While Fighter Command largely remained the main target for Luftwaffe attention during the Battle of Britain, the RAF's Bomber and Coastal Commands had equally vital roles to play in the country's defence. Fighter aircraft alone would never be enough to resist a full-blown invasion, and a striking force was required to bring direct pressure on targets in occupied Europe. In this way Bomber Command continued to attack German industries, undertaking raids on French ports where Germany was assembling its invasion fleet and reducing the threat posed by the Luftwaffe by targeting their airfields and aircraft factories. The RAF's Coastal Command also played an important role by carrying out anti-invasion patrols, thereby providing vital intelligence on German units and shipping positioned along the French coast. They would also join Bomber Command in attacking German-held ports and industrial targets.

But the RAF was not fighting alone. In his book *The People's War*, Angus Calder astutely observed that while the role of 'The Few' pilots should be praised, it would be more accurate to suggest that 'never had so few warriors owed so much to so many... besides the pilots, many un-praised heroes exhausted themselves in maintaining the brittle and intricate structure of defence'.

Indeed, huge numbers of people worked collectively to defend Britain. Ground crew – including riggers, fitters, armourers and repair and maintenance engineers – looked after the aircraft. Factory

(Left) A formation of Heinkel He 111 bombers, photographed in 1940.

workers ensured that aircraft production levels were maintained. The Observer Corps tracked incoming raids, with their tens of thousands of volunteers ensuring that the observation posts were continuously manned around the clock. Anti-aircraft gunners, searchlight operators and barrage balloon crews all played similarly vital roles in Britain's defence. Members of the Women's Auxiliary Air Force (WAAF) and Women's Royal Naval Service (WRNS) served as radar operators and worked as plotters, tracking aerial activity in their respective operations rooms. The Local Defence Volunteers (later named the Home Guard) had been set up in May 1940 as a last line of defence against German invasion, and by July nearly 1.5 million men had enrolled in this force to 'do their bit'. The Battle of Britain was in every sense a 'People's War'. While at this point in the battle Fighter Command were at the sharp end of Germany's attacks in the skies, this would change over the coming months as the greater emphasis on bombing moved the fight more into the civilian sphere.

But in terms of the strain and constant pressure in meeting the Luftwaffe's aerial attacks, it was the Fighter Command pilots who certainly bore the brunt at this stage in the battle. The persistent daily combat was both physically draining and intensely nerve-racking, yet many pilots recalled that while in the air their professionalism and determination took over to banish such concerns. It was, rather, on the ground that anxiety tended to develop, as Richard Hillary described when discussing how he took to the air to engage the enemy for the very first time.

> I climbed into the cockpit of my plane and felt an empty sensation of suspense in the pit of my stomach. For one second time seemed to stand still and I stared blankly in front of me. I knew that that morning I was to kill for the first time. That I might be killed or in any way injured did not occur to me. Later, when we were losing pilots regularly, I did consider it in an abstract way when on the ground; but once in the air, never. I know it could not happen to me. I suppose every pilot knows that, knows it cannot happen to him; even when he is taking off for the last time, when he will not return, he knows that he cannot be killed. I wondered idly what he was like, this man I would kill. Was he young, was he fat, would he die with the Führer's name on his lips, or would he die alone, in that last moment conscious of himself as a man? I would never know. Then I was being strapped in, my mind automatically checking the controls, and we were off.

The phenomena of 'flying stress' – what we would today probably refer to as post-traumatic stress disorder (PTSD) – was recognised by the RAF commanders and they made provisions to prevent it, within the limitations of the situation. In August, Dowding ordered a period of at least 24 hours' rest for each pilot every week, while the system of

rotating pilots between squadrons similarly provided some opportunity for respite from the constant action. But there were still instances when built-up stress erupted into moments of uncontrollable fear for some pilots, as once witnessed by Flight Lieutenant Denys Gillam.

> We had one pilot that went to pieces on the ground just as he was getting into his aeroplane. The doctor went up to this chap and hit him hard on the chin, knocking him out. He had to do that. The chap was making a drama out of taking off and one couldn't have that in front of all the other pilots.

As the battle developed, so too did the tactics adopted by either side. Fighter Command in particular was highly adaptive to the changing nature of the German attacks against them. Aircraft bases were moved further inland, away from the more dangerous coastal areas, while satellite airfields were increasingly used as support and protection for the larger ones. Spitfires and Hurricanes from 10 and 12 Groups were largely kept back to protect the airfields, while pilots of 11 Group were directed against the raiders.

British pilots were soon instructed to only engage the Luftwaffe over land, since clusters of German fighters would often linger over the Channel in order to draw the British defenders out into an area where the Germans could isolate them and enjoy greater manoeuvrability. For similar reasons, the British were also encouraged to attack the German bombers first and avoid fighters wherever possible. In recognition of the different strengths of each type of aircraft, Spitfires would usually engage with the escorting fighters, while Hurricanes hunted down the bomber force. This goes some way to explaining the different loss ratios for each aircraft: proportionately, more Spitfires were destroyed than any other type.

There was also the British strategy of using large 'Big Wing' formations of multiple squadrons of fighter aircraft as a means to strike at approaching German aircraft with maximum force, which led to some animosity between the RAF commanders. Championed by Wing Commander Douglas Bader and supported by his commander Leigh-Mallory, such a tactic proved controversial because organising such large formations could take time and in some cases would lead to delays in mobilising aircraft. It also caused confusion for those on the ground plotting the position of enemy raids and friendly fighters. Opponents of the idea, such as Keith Park, argued that concentrating so much attention on enemy fighters would risk allowing bombers to continue to their targets unimpeded. In the event, the Big Wing concept was seldom put into operation anyway and could boast limited success. In the second half of October, Bader's squadrons based at Duxford managed only ten such sorties, which resulted in only a single enemy plane being shot down.

Squadron Leader Brian 'Sandy' Lane, the commanding officer of No. 19 Squadron RAF (shown in the corner, looking at the camera), relaxes with some of his pilots in the crew room at Manor Farm, Fowlmere, in September 1940.

'The Big Wing'. Formations of Hurricanes climb through the clouds to intercept an enemy formation reported to be heading for London, September 1940.

Despite the Luftwaffe's targeting of air stations, the RAF communications held up well throughout the battle, with sector operations rooms only being put out of action on three occasions. Chain Home stations also remained largely unscathed, mainly because the Germans failed to recognise the importance of these installations. The relatively simple nature of the Chain Home stations also meant that they were difficult to put out of action for long.

Yet the policy of targeting airfields and associated sites inevitably led to collateral damage inflicted on civilian areas. It was not just the RAF who had to put up with the attacks, but ordinary civilians too. George King, who worked as a shorthand writer in the law courts, lived in the southern outskirts of London and commuted to the City during the day. He kept a regular diary, carefully recording each day's war news for the sake of his absent son, who had been captured at Dunkirk. Invariably, the news would concern the latest bombing raids.

> Thursday, 15 August. As regards war news, Hitler's battle for Britain seems to be starting, or developing. Heavy air attacks have been made along the south coast, resulting in the loss of 205 Jerry planes, and 50 (not all the pilots) of ours. This is grand, and our chappies

have their tails right up. Apparently, they have employed anything up to 500 planes for each attack, but they have not broken through. May the day soon come when our force is even equal to their numbers. They won't be able to fly at all.

Sunday, 18 August. All the week the enemy have been bombing many parts of the country, but their losses have been tremendous – over 400 planes down, against under 100 of our pilots lost. Our fellows have been magnificent. The only black spot was the raid on Croydon, warning of which was not given, when it might well have been. We were at Bletchingley and saw and heard the whole battle in the distance, and three of the machines were brought down quite near us; saw them hit the ground, and the rising smoke.

Had to break off my diary because we have had another raid; it lasted about half an hour, and we all went under the stairs, where Biddy was quite good. It was a devil of a racket, in the course of which a machine gun chase went on over the house. Well, after a bite to eat, I went on duty [as an ARP warden]... and got the job of stopping sightseers, guarding craters and looking for unexploded bombs. The nearest to us fell... a distance I estimate at 400 yards as the crow flies... altogether round here about a dozen bombs fell, thank goodness not large ones. Some of the houses were knocked about, but I have not heard of one casualty... Had just finished a cup of tea when there was another warning, but this time our chappies must have beaten them off, because the sky seemed stiff with Hurricanes and Spitfires.

Tuesday, 20 August. The weather seems to have broken a little, and it has not been good for flying. Of course, we are glad of the respite here, but there seems to have been some damage in other parts of the country. However, the general opinion seems to be that last week marked a definite stage in the Battle for Britain; the Germans now know that their Air Force is not invincible. Their losses in the raid in this district were 144, including one brought down by rifle fire by the Home Guard.

The country was clearly becoming used to the regular attacks from the air. But the worst was yet to come.

Chapter Six

THE BOMBING OF CITIES, SEPTEMBER 1940

Continuing to believe their inaccurate intelligence reports, the Luftwaffe felt towards the end of August 1940 that the RAF were so close to being finished that the next phase of the operation against Britain could begin. This would involve attacking the rest of the country but concentrating on industrial, military and transport targets. Effectively a continuation of the original plan for breaking British resolve, while also preparing the way for a potential invasion, this would involve abandoning attacks specifically on Fighter Command airfields in order to widen the nature of the assault.

The new infrastructure targets for Luftwaffe bombing tended to be located in and around major urban areas, and an inevitable consequence of this would therefore be much greater civilian casualties. Heavy bombing began on the night of 19/20 August, targeting cities such as Bristol, Liverpool, Birmingham and the outskirts of London. By the end of the month London suburbs such as Finchley, St Pancras, Wood Green and the Old Kent Road had also sustained bomb damage and a high level of casualties. Throughout July some 258 civilians had been killed across the country, but with the new Luftwaffe strategy this had risen by the end of August to 1,075. These numbers included 392 women and 136 children. George King continued to carefully record each day's war news in his diary.

> Sunday, 25 August. For the first time a lone machine got into London and there seems to have been some damage done round St Paul's. However, our defences (thanks to the handful of gallant lads in the Air Force) are holding, and I am getting much more bucked about things. I freely confess that for weeks after Dunkirk I thought we were in Queer Street, but thanks to the German passion for thorough organisation, he did not invade us. It could have been done then with success, but there would be an entirely different story to tell now!

> Tuesday, 27 August. Rather a bad night... The sirens went at 9.15pm and we did not get the 'all-clear' till 4 o'clock this morning. To start with, we three retired to the Gillet's shelter, and I stuck it until 2am but then came into the house and fell asleep on the bed, and the 'all clear' woke me up. One must have a spot of sleep when there is work to do. The papers have described it as 'a nuisance raid', but it is rather more than that. The Jerries want to find out what they can do at night time over London. But they were up at least 20,000 ft and could not have seen anything, and did not even have the satisfaction of finding out exactly where the batteries are. Three were brought down, one at Warlingham.

> Wednesday, 28 August. I had hardly finished writing my entry last night... at 9.30 when the sirens went, and down into the shelter we had to go till 12 o'clock. No stuff was dropped here and there were only one or two planes. Well we were just settling down to sleep at

(Page 152–153) Battle of Britain: The Burning of the City by Joseph Gray, 1940. A view from the south bank of the River Thames towards St Paul's Cathedral and the City of London, shrouded in smoke as a result of German air raids.

Two Dornier Do 217 bombers fly over the Plumstead sewer bank, Crossness pumping station and the Royal Arsenal on 7 September 1940.

12.30 when the blessed things went again, and we came back to the house just before 2 o'clock. So we managed a bit of sleep, but not enough for my slogging commercial arbitration today.

By now, the irritation felt from lack of sleep and the regular interruptions to normal life were becoming quite obvious in Mr King's diary.

> Saturday, 31 August. It is getting almost impossible to find time to do what one wants; there are so many air raid warnings, which last anything from an hour upwards. Then during the all clear times one tries to get the really necessary jobs done. Also, during the last week we have had very little sleep.

On the final day of August 1940 the young Donald Bruce was at his family home in Shooters Hill, near Woolwich in south-east London. He had enlisted in the RAF as aircrew, but was currently on deferred service while waiting for his training to begin. That afternoon he would witness a daylight engagement between German fighter bombers and the RAF's Spitfires.

> It was around teatime and a raid was in progress and an aerial battle was taking place in the haze above. I was in the garden and heard the fighters diving and letting off bursts of machine gun fire, in fact empty cartridge cases cascaded into the garden and when I picked some up they were still warm. Suddenly there was the noise of a plane diving at great speed and then a plane broke through the haze heading straight for the deck. Its wheels were down and at first sight I thought it was a Ju 87, it turned very slowly in a lazy sort of spin and as its silhouette appeared I recognised it as a Spitfire. It had obviously been shot up and its hydraulics were damaged, hence the wheels down attitude. As it neared the ground the wheels flapped a little and then just before it reached the balloon barrage the engine seemed to blow up and disintegrate, it had also stopped the slow spin at this stage and was straight as a die for the deck. It disappeared from my sight behind some houses and crashed on Woolwich Common. The pilot was either dead or unconscious before he hit the ground, as at no time did he appear to attempt to control the plane.

With encounters such as this, the bombing of London had clearly already begun when Hitler made a speech on 4 September in which he implied that Britain's capital would now be targeted in retaliation for the recent British bombing of Berlin on 25/26 August. This in turn had been retaliation for the earlier German attacks on London, although the Berlin raid was actually quite small in scale and inflicted negligible damage. Its impact on German complacency, however, was arguably much more significant. While Hitler had made the deliberate decision to draw attention to London as a bombing target, the overall German

(Page 156) Londoners sleep on the escalators of the Underground while taking shelter overnight from German air raids in 1940. Few enjoyed the experience; as the nights wore on and the bombing intensified, stations would become increasingly crowded, and with no proper sanitation, the smell could be awful.

(Page 157) Gas Mask by William Brealey, 1939. Expectations of a gas attack from the air were high at the beginning of the war, and ARP wardens, as depicted in this painting, were appropriately equipped to handle the potential threat.

(Right) An Aerial Battle by Francis Dodd, 1940.

This remarkable photograph, taken on 18 September 1940, shows a pattern of contrails (or condensation trails) left by British and German aircraft high up in the sky.

Coast Defence Battery, September 1940
by Barnett Freedman, 1941.

The Bombing of Cities, September 1940   163

strategy for the campaign remained unchanged and they continued to follow the plans put in place some months earlier in order to break Britain's resolve.

While still waiting for his RAF training to begin, Donald Bruce had taken up employment as a clerk at the nearby Woolwich Arsenal, a key target for enemy bombing. The experience of being on the receiving end of German bombs was a novelty for some, but over the next months and years it would come to be almost second nature in its regularity and persistence.

> The air raid warning went in the afternoon and I can remember a feeling of slight insecurity as now that the raids had intensified I had no great desire to be in close proximity to a prime target. We filed into the shelter which was a long, narrow concrete affair... above ground and covered with a protective covering of earth. There were long, narrow, slatted wooden seats running the length of the shelter... I was at the far end away from the door and when we heard the first bombs dropping they were close enough to be disconcerting and for the first time in an air raid I began to feel afraid. My feelings weren't strengthened when one man at the door end of the shelter rushed out in panic bellowing and shouting, more bombs were dropping nearer and some of the men near the door rushed out to drag him back in and they had to sit on him to hold him down. This character incidentally never came back after the raid, he cleared off out of London. I had up to that time always assumed that adults were like my father who stoically endured all situations 'like a grown up', and I think that this incident had more of a profound effect on me than the bombs did.

> Whether this showed in my face I'll never know, but an old man I had seen in the carriage shop occasionally came and sat next to me and in a quiet voice started to tell me how he had travelled all over France and Spain and the adventures he had experienced. Whilst he was talking in this quiet, controlled manner the next wave came over and started to drop their sticks very close, we heard the whistle of the bombs and the shelter rocked and jumped as though it were floating on water (this was a peculiar sensation that I experienced with later night raids, a stick landed near my brother's bungalow one night in 1940 and although the bombs didn't burst, the ground seemed to sway and the bungalow swayed with it). These bombs were extremely close and I think everybody in the shelter was pretty shaken, but I was very thankful for the old man who had helped to calm me whilst my hands were gripping the slats of the seats, with the knuckles all white.

Despite the high civilian casualty rates which resulted from the Luftwaffe bombing, it is important to remember that bombing by either side was seldom indiscriminate. Both the RAF and Luftwaffe chose only

(Right) Eileen Dunne, aged three, sits in bed with her doll at Great Ormond Street Hospital for Sick Children, after being injured during an air raid on London in September 1940. This famous photograph was taken by Cecil Beaton.

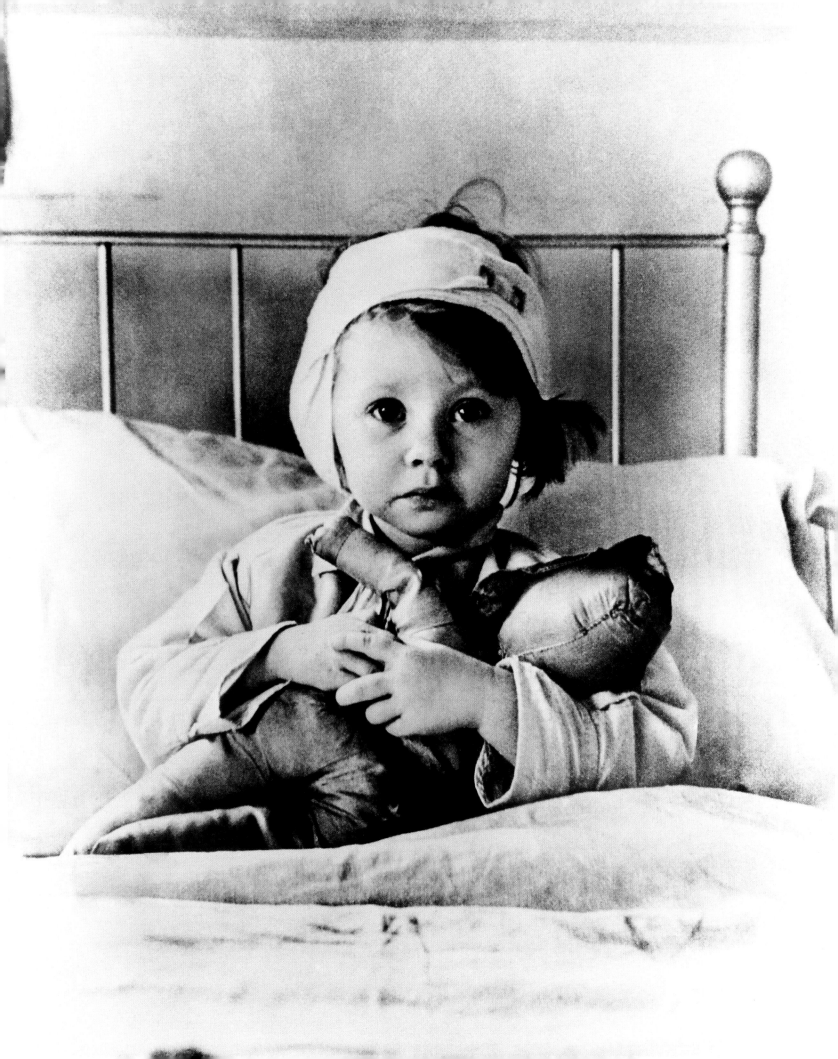

Shelter Drawing by Henry Moore, 1941.

(Right) A House Collapsing on Two Firemen, Shoe Lane, London, EC4 by Leonard Rosoman, 1940

Leonard Rosoman

Battle of Britain: The First Blitz
by Joseph Gray, 1940.

war-essential targets rather than mounting deliberate attacks on civilian areas, and they operated under what were almost identical instructions to hit only military and economic objectives. Neither air force was permitted to mount terror attacks for the sake of it. German bombers were told to attack only when they had good visual contact with the target, and otherwise to bring their bombs back for a future attempt rather than to dump them on suburban areas. The one exception to this rule related to London, which could be attacked on moonless nights since it offered a large target area in which something useful was bound to be hit. Yet despite these precautionary guidelines it was obviously impossible to avoid civilian casualties and fatalities, which progressively grew in number.

Beginning with the first daylight raid by 348 bombers on Saturday, 7 September, London was continually bombed by day and night. From this date until 5 October, when daylight bombing petered out due to the heavy losses sustained by the Luftwaffe's bomber force, Britain experienced 35 major attacks, including 18 on London. This marked the beginning of the Blitz, a shortening of the German term Blitzkrieg or 'lightning war' which evoked the quick and deadly fashion in which Germany had attacked Poland, the Low Countries and France. As an expression to refer to the bombing of Britain, it described the violent, sudden attacks which happened repeatedly, day after day and then night after night, in an attempt to break the civilian population. Throughout the eight months of German air raids suffered by the country, from September 1940 to May of the following year, some 43,000 civilians were killed. This number would form almost half of Britain's total civilian deaths for the entire war. The damage inflicted to homes and businesses should also not be forgotten; one in every six Londoners was made homeless at some point, with 1.1 million houses and flats being destroyed or seriously damaged.

German bombers would usually arrive in three waves, and Fighter Command squadrons were then progressively sent after them, climbing to as high an altitude as they could in order to have the tactical advantage. British fighters would often give false height references over wireless in order to fool their German opponents. On 21 September standing patrols were introduced to intercept bombers much more quickly, with Hurricanes flying at bomber altitude and Spitfires at a height above enemy fighters in readiness to engage them. This new technique resulted in a reduced rate of loss for the British, while the Luftwaffe bomber force suffered much higher casualties. The Germans responded over time by flying at ever-increasing altitudes, in order to avoid anti-aircraft fire as well as gain a height advantage over the RAF fighters attempting to intercept them. As gunner J W Clark recalled:

> In general, it was very noticeable that as time passed the German planes flew higher. At first, during July, heights were usually below 12,000 but in September rarely under 20,000 and often nearer

30,000. Later still, in October and November, the RAF kept a patrol of about twelve Spitfires, almost constantly up and down the coast at between 30,000 and 32,000 feet.

During the initial week of attacks on London, the German bomber force lost some 199 aircraft. For the pilots of Fighter Command, the days which followed throughout September would mark the most intense period for them in terms of constantly responding to bombing raids and incoming fighters. Pilot Officer John Carpenter flew with No. 222 Squadron based at Hornchurch, and was a veteran of the Norwegian campaign. Despite much success in the Battle of Britain, Carpenter was eventually shot down and sent to hospital, from where he wrote home to his parents.

> I suppose I had better tell you how I got here in the first place. I had just attacked an Me 109 and was breaking away at some pretty speed when (I did not know at the time) I was hit by one of our own 3.7 anti-aircraft shells. I am not shooting a line when I say that the machine just disappeared from under me in one big BANG! and, with a bit of good luck that must go with that watch of yours, I found myself propelled clear of the aeroplane. I pulled the ripcord and started my grateful descent to earth. I must have got a hit over the head somewhere but my eyes just would not function. Considering all the good luck I have had it was not surprising that it had to change, for I landed in the hardest, knobbliest and most spiteful tree you could find; it was a kind of nut tree. Needless to say, I was carted off to hospital with many scratches and cuts, where they chloroformed me and did a lot of needlework. But now I am glad to say, having recovered from the effects of chloroform, which made me sick as a dog, I hope to be able to get up soon.

The enemy bomber formations grew larger and more deadly, and it was clear that the Luftwaffe were throwing everything they had at Britain. Gunner Clark noted in his diary the remarkable scale of these raids.

> This evening, just after tea, the war suddenly woke up. I was off duty and up at the huts when the alarm sounded. The raid developed well and truly and never have I seen so many heavy bombers in the sky at the same time. There must have been literally hundreds, as they came over in formations of 30 or 40, and there were more formations than I could count. There was every type known to us... They mostly flew very high, but at the same time a few Heinkels raided the harbour, probably to attract our attention. We heard several salvoes of bombs whistle down... Next day we heard that London was their target, and that there were 2,000 casualties and heaven knows how much damage.

This period, covering the week following 7 September, would prove to be the most decisive period of the Battle of Britain. This was recognised

(Left) A film still from gun camera footage taken by Pilot Officer Keith 'Skeets' Ogilvie of No. 609 Squadron RAF showing a Dornier Do 17Z under attack on 15 September 1940. The aircraft was later abandoned by its crew; it flew on until it was rammed over central London by Sergeant Ray Holmes of No. 504 Squadron RAF, resulting in its crash on Victoria station. Having baled out, the German pilot was attacked by civilians and died of his injuries the following day.

Soldiers guard part of the wreckage of a
Heinkel He 111 which blew up and crashed
over southern England, 1940.

by George King, who continued to record his impressions of the battle through regular diary entries.

> Wednesday, 11 September. We are told we are coming to the decisive days of the war. Our grand air force have inflicted heavy losses on the enemy, and salvation has been given to us by a handful of young men. The next fortnight, or even the next few days, will show whether Hitler will attempt invasion. In my humble opinion, if every soul does his or her job as they have been doing during the past few weeks, there is no question but that it is the beginning of the end of those foul beasts.

> Saturday, 14 September. We are still living in pretty hectic times... but seem to have found some answer to the devastating night raids which go on from about 8 in the evening till 5.30 the next morning. London is now plastered with guns of all kinds, and the barrage is simply terrific. It keeps on waking me up from my bed under the stairs, but the great thing is that one feels something is being done. Another item of war news is that the devils dive-bombed Buckingham Palace yesterday, and did a lot of damage. But the King and Queen went out afterwards on a tour of south London to sympathise with the people.

During this short period the Luftwaffe actually lost 298 aircraft, including 99 fighters, while Fighter Command lost 120. The greatest damage was inflicted on Sunday, 15 September, which would come to be known as Battle of Britain Day to reflect its importance as one of the deciding moments of the campaign. Around 1,500 aircraft fought in the skies that day until dusk, including more than 300 German bombers plus a heavy fighter escort which attacked in three waves, to be met by more than 300 Spitfires and Hurricanes. 158 German bombers reached London, but they were unsuccessful in damaging their intended targets due to poor visibility. 34 bombers were ultimately destroyed, 20 were more extensively damaged and 26 fighters were shot down. David Cox recalled the pivotal day of 15 September from the perspective of a Spitfire pilot with No. 19 Squadron, based at RAF Duxford.

> We went off in the morning. There were two raids that day: the lunchtime and the teatime. They said the Germans were trying to spoil our Sunday lunch and tea – which they effectively did. This was midday and we – the wing – intercepted a raid just south of London. Again, we were taking the Messerschmitt 109s on. And after the first pass or two I suddenly saw a Dornier below me. I made an attack but he got into cloud. I had plenty of ammunition, so I flew south a little bit and to my right I saw six single-engine aircraft, which I thought were Hurricanes. And we'd always been told that you shouldn't fly around on your own, you should always try and join up with any friendly aircraft. But it was the angle I was looking at: they turned towards me and I turned towards them and suddenly found

they were six 109s. Which you might say was slightly embarrassing! We were on about the same level, but four of the 109s dived away — I saw nothing more of them. Of the other two, one climbed up behind me and one climbed up above me in front, and the one behind attacked and I turned very violently and he just carried straight on and I didn't see him again. But the one who'd been above me, I turned and he was coming at right angles and I fired with a 90-degree deflection, saw strikes on his aircraft, and he then went down through some broken cloud and crashed near Crowborough.

Keeping the score back on the ground was George King, who resumed his diary entries for this fateful week of the battle in order to sum up its climax.

Sunday, 15 September. There have been two big scraps over London today, and 50 Jerry bombers are down. I saw one coming down myself. They had another shot at the Palace, damn them, and damaged the Queen's apartments.

Tuesday, 17 September. Those figures above have to be amended… there were 185 bombers brought down, and that is the record day for the air force.

The Luftwaffe was now experiencing a huge 25 per cent loss rate, which in the longer term would prove unsustainable. Following another mass daylight raid of 70 bombers on 18 September, which similarly resulted in heavy losses, the raids were switched to mainly night-time. While the Germans could now take advantage of the cover of night for their operations, the inhabitants of British cities could at least live their lives during daylight hours without the frequent interruption of air raid alerts.

The date 15 September also happened to have been the one set many weeks before for the start of Operation Sea Lion. On 30 August this had been delayed slightly to 20 September, but at a conference on 14 September the German leadership began to accept for the first time that their intelligence sources had been overconfident in predicting the fall of Britain's defences. The Germans had clearly not achieved air superiority, and three days later they postponed the invasion indefinitely. Sea Lion could be reconsidered the following year, if Britain had not succumbed to the continued German bombing campaign before then. In the meantime Britain could instead be challenged through the fighting going on in the Mediterranean theatre and the eastern Atlantic. The Luftwaffe was still given free rein to continue their ceaseless air attacks over England until British resolve cracked, and in those terms the Battle of Britain would therefore continue, with a renewed emphasis on bombing.

Chapter Seven

THE CONTINUED BLITZ, LATE SEPTEMBER–DECEMBER 1940

The Battle of Britain was now firmly a battle of attrition, with the Luftwaffe tasked with continuing to wear away at their foe until British resistance collapsed. The 'quick' route to a German invasion through destruction of Fighter Command had been thwarted, but the long-haul task of beating their opponent remained. While the Germans held off from a deliberate policy of inducing mass civilian panic, this next phase of the battle would see much more indiscriminate bombing through the adoption of more widely scattered attacks. Legitimate military and economic targets were still the rule, however, although residential areas inevitably suffered as a result. The administrative and government centres of central London were added to the target list, which led to a greater emphasis on attacking the capital city, while the regularity of the bombing contributed to the process of wearing down the British population. But by involving the British populace in the war to such an extent, the Germans effectively had scored an own-goal. Determination to beat them was now at an all-time high, with fighter pilots like Ronald Berry inspired to fight back even harder than before.

Air raid wardens were issued with steel helmets. These were similar to the head protection issued to soldiers in the First World War and protected the wearer from falling shrapnel or debris. Steel helmets were also issued to firefighters, police officers and other members of civil defence services, and they soon became a recognisable symbol of authority.

(Right) This stirrup pump and hose was used to put out small fires, often started by incendiary bombs. The equipment would be used by two people – one working the pump, which stood in a bucket of water, and a second holding the hose and nozzle to direct the water.

(Pages 176–177) Sleepers in the Crypt by Edward Ardizzone, 1941.

> I do know that when I saw Heinkels just unleashing their load onto the poor populace of London, it had the effect on me of making me hopping mad. And I think that from that moment on, I had the feeling that there was something much more serious than just having dogfights in the air going on. And perhaps from then on I think it sunk in a bit more solidly than it had done before at that sort of bombing. I would think there's a word you get into it: bloodlust, I suppose. I think that some people don't like killing anybody. I never thought of killing anybody. I just wanted to shoot them down. That's how I felt about it.

The methods of bombing were changing too. The Germans regularly dropped many clusters of smaller incendiary bombs, with the aim of starting fires, damaging property and creating a trail for other bomb aimers to follow. Cluster bombs held around 600 incendiaries each, and some of the smaller bombs would operate with a delayed fuse, extending the threat following the 'all clear' signal. Popular entertainers of the day such as Will Hay starred in government information films to keep the public alert to the air raid danger and tell them what to do when encountering threats such as unexploded bombs, yet people did not always follow such advice accurately, as bank clerk Joan Varley remembered.

> The morning after they first dropped incendiaries, we went into the bank and discovered one on the upper floor. We'd never seen one before. It wasn't very big but it was plainly a device and there was a hole in the wall where it had entered. It was found by one of the bank cashiers, rather a stately, stiff kind of man, and we were saying, 'Pick it up, get rid of it,' so he picked it up and put it in a fire bucket full of water. He was taking it to the lift but we said, 'No! No!

You mustn't go in the lift. If you blow up the lift we won't be able to get out!' So we made the poor man walk down the stairs, where he handed it to an air raid warden. We found out afterwards that the last thing you should do with an incendiary is to put it in a bucket of water [the bomb contained magnesium, which water would not extinguish].

Large parachute mines were used too, dropped over docks in order to damage shipping. The rules of engagement over London on moonless nights were relaxed as well, allowing more indiscriminate bombing. Such measures reveal a gradual abandonment by the Germans of any pretence that civilians would not become targets of the campaign. Close to 43,000 people in total would be killed throughout the Battle of Britain and Blitz, stretching the idea of 'collateral damage' to its very limits.

John Sweetland was 13 years old in 1940, and lived with his family in a small flat in Marylebone, London. The distant life-and-death aerial dog fights in the skies above London were a regular form of entertainment for some, particularly schoolchildren, who were out of range of the dangers. But as bombing raids intensified and grew nearer and nearer to home, the exhilaration inevitably took a more realistic and sinister turn.

Living in a first floor flat at the end of a communal balcony gave a clear view eastwards... across Euston, Kings Cross and St Pancras Stations, and in the direction of Bethnal Green and Bow, thus ensuring a grandstand view of the August and September air battles. Neighbours on our floor would congregate outside our front door to cheer at the tops of their voices through the crackle of the machine gun fire and wonder at the aircraft vapour trails in the clear, blue skies. There was even greater excitement and cheering when a fighter plane was shot down, but I thought it to be a Hurricane. A 'drying room' on the top floor of our block provided another vantage point. On one occasion that September I was able to see a large formation of aircraft flying low across Hampstead, perhaps to bomb Hendon aerodrome... On the 7th September came our greatest show without harm when the docks and East End were ablaze with enormous fires and columns of smoke, all to be viewed from our front door. From that time onwards, things would be different.

Now at the end of the first week in September, we were becoming accustomed to the sirens and spasmodic night attacks just beginning. The daylight bombing had seemed bad enough but when the planes returned just after 8pm to continue their attack throughout the night we thought of the newsreels we had seen and even that the government would sue for peace. Being nearly fourteen years old I had found my recent experiences exciting. After all, it was just like watching a film. Only happening to other people

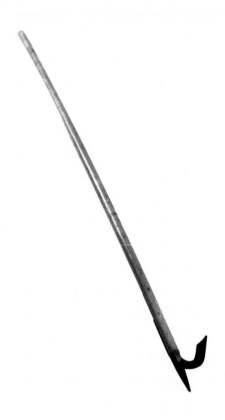

This ceiling pike is over three metres long and was used by air raid wardens when exploring bomb-damaged buildings. Wardens could use the point to give potentially unsafe ceilings a testing poke, and use the bill hook to snag and dislodge debris.

(Right) Air raid wardens were often the first link in the chain of Britain's civil defence system. Wardens worked from a network of posts which were connected to higher command by telephone or messenger. When bombing raids occurred, wardens on duty had to monitor and report bomb damage on forms like the one shown here. Such accurate information proved vital when saving lives and protecting important buildings from damage.

WARDEN'S REPORT FORM.

Form of Report to Report Centres.

AIR RAID DAMAGE (Commence report with these words)

Designation of Reporting Agent
    (e.g., Warden's Post No.   )

Position of occurrence

Type of bombs : —HE/Incendiary/Poison Gas

Approx. No. of Casualties : —
    (If any trapped under wreckage, say so)

If fire, say so : —

Damage to mains : —Water /Coal Gas /Overhead electric cables/Sewers

Names of Roads blocked

Position of any unexploded bombs

Time of occurrence (approx.)

Services already on the spot or coming : —

Remarks : —

ORIGINAL ⎫ These words are for use with a report sent by messenger.
DUPLICATE ⎭   Delete whichever does not apply.

The Tube: October 1940 by Feliks
Topolski, 1940.

(Left) Finding an Unexploded Bomb,
Barton Street, London SW1 by
Duncan Oppenheim, 1940.

with me as a spectator from our balcony vantage point outside our front door… On the following day, Sunday the 8th, our view to the east was shrouded in a hazy backdrop of different shades of grey to black in a great smoky pall, I could even smell it. Few residents were seen to go out and those that did were subdued with shock and disbelief. From that weekend the raids continued both night and day for the remainder of September.

For those living in Britain, fears of an imminent invasion were gradually replaced by a test of endurance. Over 8 months there were 127 large-scale night raids across the country, of which 72 were on London. The Blitz saw 46,000 tons of high-explosive bombs and 110,000 incendiary bombs dropped, leading to the destruction of more than 2 million homes, well over half located in London. While the Blitz was a nationwide campaign which targeted many cities and ports across the country, it was inevitable that London, as the largest and most significant, would receive the greatest attention from the enemy.

The bombing of British cities led to the emergence of what would come to be defined as the 'Blitz spirit': the will to carry on against the odds, to maintain a semblance of normality within the chaos and uncertainty of the bombing. The idea of 'business as usual' became popularised, partly as a defiant stance by the civilian population against the enemy, but also out of necessity to keep businesses going and regular life continuing. Throughout September and October, John Sweetland's father was doing night work, leaving the 13-year-old and his mother alone in their Marylebone flat.

> My parents didn't believe in air raid shelters, holding the philosophy that 'if we were going, we would all go together'. Neither would mother consider going to bed during a raid. Therefore the nights without father were spent trying to sleep on the living room floor in makeshift beds, fully clothed ready for an emergency, as much under the dining table as was possible, the 'tin box' containing family papers, some cash, etc. beside mother. The main light, a small three bulb chandelier hung from a ceiling rose, was kept on, for no sleep could be had unless complete exhaustion took over. We just lay there with the cacophony of the planes, bombs and guns about us, feeling the building sway when a bomb fell close and watching the chandelier become more of a pendulum as it swung back and forth with the building, the bulbs dimming, flickering and sometimes going out altogether. Mother lay there terrified, an expression of agony on her face. I was little better.

> The sounds of the Blitz were distinctive. Sometimes we would be made aware that the raiders were on their way as the BBC radio programmes suddenly became indistinct, bringing on a very unwelcome anticipation. Soon then the first siren would be heard, perhaps away in the distance. Then others would join in

(Right) A man and woman asleep under blankets in the Tube tunnel at Liverpool Street Underground shelter in November 1940. After so many people used the Underground as an informal refuge, the authorities moved past their initial reluctance and started turning disused tunnels into deep shelters. These were sometimes fitted with bunk beds and ARP stations to organise the masses who sought safety.

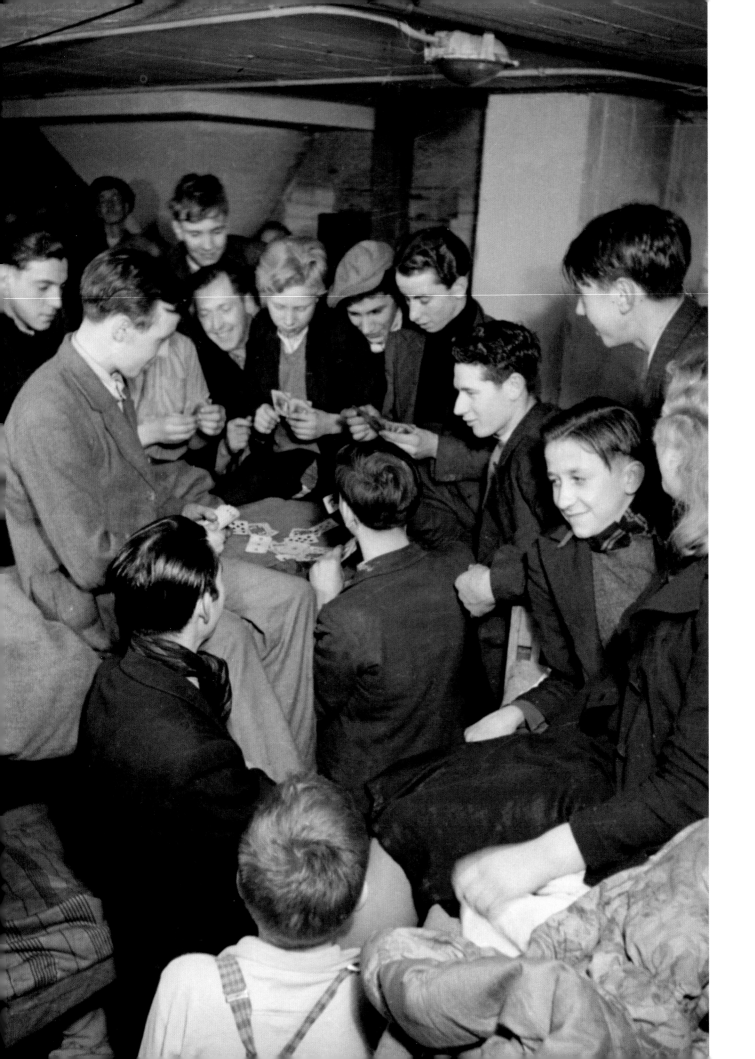

sounding nearer and nearer until our very own siren on the roof of Albany Street police station would join in. The guns too had their different sounds. Our local battery on Primrose Hill would let out a thunderous roar and sometimes a mobile gun stopped in Cumberland Market would let fly with a tremendous bang. The soft 'crumps' of exploding anti-aircraft shells were quite mild, accompanied by the falling shrapnel which gave out metallic rings as pieces hit the hard ground or bounced off or rolled along roofs before it too 'pinged' to the ground. A shower of incendiaries sounded like a hundred cricket balls struck by bats, and as for falling bombs, sometimes a long drawn out whistle, but a 'close one' would give an ever increasing rushing sound.

Any initial public panic exhibited when the bombing had started earlier in September had died down by the end of the month once morale stiffened. Yet despite such an overall tenacious attitude, those suffering from the regular attacks still felt considerable fear. There was very little one could do, as John Sweetland recalled, other than try to maintain some semblance of a normal life among the air raid precautions and regular disruption.

I would read, draw, listen to the radio, sometimes searching the airwaves to relieve the boredom, and when feeling very daring... listen to William Joyce speaking from Germany for a short while... In late September mother and I had been invited twice when father was working evenings into a neighbour's flat for an evening sing song to lift our spirits, but communal tea and biscuits accompanied by a hearty chorus of Roll out the Barrel were not mother's forte. Occasionally, when the raids eased for a night or two we made an early visit to the cinema. When the raiders had arrived an announcement was flashed up onto the screen – 'An alert has sounded, but for patrons who wish to stay the performance will continue. Please leave quietly.' To stay could be nerve wracking, especially when things became noisy outside.

The bombing raids now arrived largely under the cover of night, and the enemy bombers were countered by Fighter Command's night fighter force of Blenheim, Defiant and Beaufighter aircraft. RDF detection and visual observation proved problematic at night, so contact with enemy bombers was often more fortuitous than deliberately planned. Anti-aircraft artillery and searchlights served as the main opposition to the bomber formations, with extra guns brought down from other areas of the country in order to protect London. Such anti-aircraft batteries claimed 337 aircraft between July and September 1940, although less than a third of these were shot down at night. It would remain exceptionally difficult to shoot down aircraft in the dark until new detection equipment was introduced later in the war. Indeed, some civilians recognised that the importance of anti-aircraft guns lay more in their contribution to self-confidence than in their actual effectiveness

(Left) Local boys play a game of cards in an air raid shelter in south-east London, November 1940.

(Pages 188–189) Air cadets and civilians examine the dinghy from a shot-down Junkers Ju 88, on display at Wood Green in London on 31 August 1940. This was probably as part of a fundraising activity.

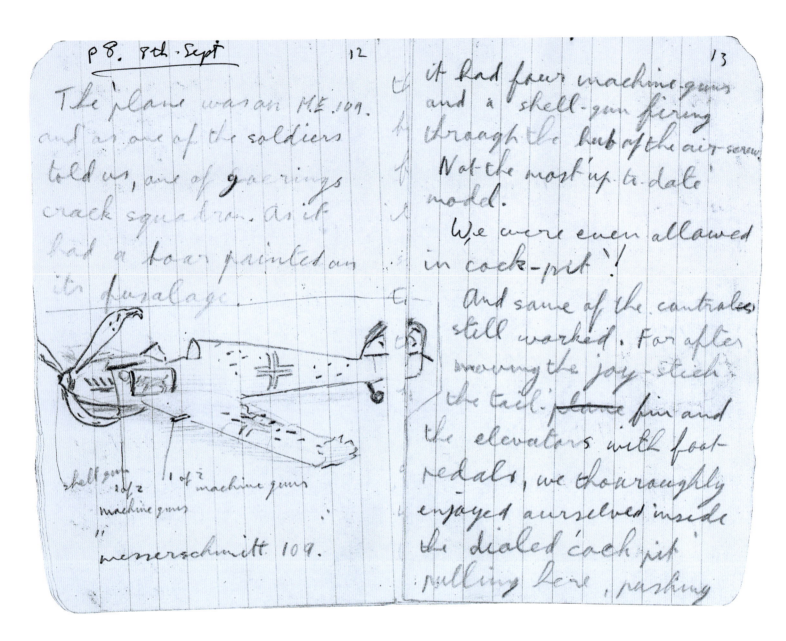

p8. 9th Sept   12

The plane was an ME.109.
and as one of the soldiers
told us, one of goerings
crack squadron. as it
had a boar painted on
its fuselage.

shell gun
1 of 2
machine guns

1 of 2 machine guns
''

messerschmitt 109.

13

it had four machine guns
and a shell-gun firing
through the hub of the air-screw.
Not the most 'up to date'
model.

We were even allowed
in cock-pit '!

And some of the controls
still worked. For after
moving the joy-stick
the tail plane fin and
the elevators with foot-
pedals, we thouraughly
enjoyed ourselves inside
the dialed 'cock pit'
pulling here, pushing

A page from schoolboy Nigel
Cameron's diary illustrating the crashed
Messerschmitt Bf 109 which he and his
friend located in the Kent countryside.

as a weapon against the bomber threat. This is certainly what Stanley Clark, an ARP messenger in London, recalled: 'The mood round our way was, why can't we hit back at the bombers? So they brought anti-aircraft guns up Gray's Inn Road for a couple of nights. But it was just morale boosting – it didn't do any good.'

Despite the great damage and high casualties inflicted by the Blitz, the bombing campaign against Britain did not prove as disastrous as was originally feared, since the Germans failed to consistently target locations of importance. Instead, they bombed wide areas, which caused extensive damage yet failed to stop the country dead in its tracks. People made repairs and carried on as best they could; 'Keep Calm and Carry On' became a popular mantra to guide civilians through the troubled times.

The morning after a raid would see schoolchildren scurrying around near bomb sites, seemingly unaware of the very real danger from unexploded bombs yet eager to find souvenirs of the war amid the rubble and debris. John Sweetland recalled how the collecting bug was satisfied by choice pieces of shrapnel.

> Even more prized was a piece of bomb casing, which was rare. Arriving on the scene just after dawn in Harrington Street where a large bomb had fallen during the night, I was delighted to find a big piece of this casing, which was too cold and jagged to be carried home by bare hands. This I guiltily hid, to be retrieved later. So, nearing the end of 1940, and much to the annoyance of my parents, I had amassed a large collection of souvenirs. Shrapnel, small bits of German aircraft, incendiary bombs in various stages of destruction, lots of incendiary fins and the base plate and rod from a 'Molotov Bread Basket', together with small sections of land mine parachute and rayon rope. My favourites were the nose cones from anti-aircraft shells in brass and aluminium with strange numbers and graduated marks upon them. These cones were very much sought after and entailed a slow, painstaking walk on Saturday and Sunday mornings over the grass in Regent's Park, looking for the small tell-tale hole from which they could be prised. My worst indignity of the time was to be confronted by two rough looking adults in the park who demanded that I hand over an excellent example for themselves.

Even better experiences were open to children living outside of the larger towns or cities. Fourteen-year-old Nigel Cameron lived in Herne Bay, Kent, and was perfectly located to witness the height of the Battle of Britain from the perspective of the countryside. The diary entries that he scribbled in a small notebook serve as the perfect illustration of how some civilians, and schoolboys in particular, embraced the battle as a thrilling event which provided numerous opportunities for amusement.

An Italian Fiat CR 42 biplane fighter which
crash-landed at Orford Ness in Suffolk during
the Italian air force's only major daylight raid of
the Battle of Britain, on 11 November 1940. A
dozen BR.20 bombers and their escorts were
intercepted by Hurricanes of Nos. 17, 46 and
257 Squadrons RAF; the enemy force suffered
heavy losses, at no cost to the RAF, and similar
daylight raids were not repeated.

This still from gun camera footage shows tracer ammunition from a Spitfire of No. 609 Squadron RAF, flown by Flight Lieutenant J H G McArthur, hitting a Heinkel He 111 on its starboard quarter. These German aircraft were part of a large formation which attacked the Bristol Aeroplane Company's works at Filton, Bristol, just before midday on 25 September 1940.

8 September 1940. At a quarter to eight in the morning, Peter and I set out to look for a bomber which a fireman told us had crashed about three miles away. We set off and soon arrived at a place a little way from the wreck. But as the farmer said it was burnt out and not worth looking at, we cycled on. After making enquiries, we heard that another plane (German) had crashed into a tree near where we were, but that too was not worth seeing. So we went on hopefully. After asking at a farm we found a Messerschmitt which had pancaked in a field. It was in quite good condition, and we ventured towards it, expecting to be told to go away. But instead we were called by the soldiers. They were dressing and enquired of us as to who had woken us up so early, and said 'I suppose you can't give us a cup of hot tea, we're froze' to which we replied that we couldn't.

We were surprised to find that we could touch it and could do what we liked so long as we took no souvenirs. The plane was an Me 109 and, as one of the soldiers told us, one of Göring's crack squadrons as it had a boar painted on its fuselage. It had four machine-guns and a shell-gun firing through the hub of the airscrew. Not the most up to date model. We were even allowed in the cockpit! And some of the controls still worked, for after moving the joystick, the tail fins and elevators with foot pedals, we thoroughly enjoyed ourselves inside the dialled cockpit, pulling here, pushing there. Peter wrenched out the oxygen mask pipe and got away with it under his coat when the guards weren't looking. Then I managed to get his strap while I talked loudly. We got our souvenirs home safely.

While there were fewer large bomber formations to be seen during daylight hours, correspondingly bigger numbers of fighters would appear in order to continue the war of attrition against Fighter Command. Groups of fighter bombers carrying a 250-kilogram bomb each were escorted by as many as 300 fighters, with 253 such raids mounted throughout October 1940 and 235 the following month. But these daylight raids began to gradually die away as the emphasis on night bombing increased and the Luftwaffe's main consideration became more about breaking civilian resolve than destroying the RAF. The Germans finally began to realise that the ratios of aircraft and pilot losses were developing in Britain's favour. In October Fighter Command lost some 146 Hurricanes and Spitfires, while the Luftwaffe lost 365 aircraft, mainly bombers. Loss rates among Fighter Command pilots were down to only ten per cent in October and reached a new, even lower point by November. The Battle of Britain was clearly shifting in the wrong direction for a German victory.

But the bombing campaign continued, relentless in the destruction it wreaked on cities across the country. Among the locations targeted as being important industrial centres or communication hubs was the Midlands city of Coventry. Local resident Miriam Hewson wrote to her daughter on 15 October 1940, the morning after a particularly nasty raid.

(Left) This gun camera still was taken from a Spitfire flown by the commanding officer of No. 609 Squadron RAF, Squadron Leader H S Darley, as he opened fire amongst a formation of Heinkel He 111s which had just bombed the Supermarine aircraft works at Woolston, near Southampton, on 26 September 1940.

(Pages 196–197) The ruins of Coventry Cathedral two days after the German Luftwaffe air raid on the city during the night of 14 November 1940.

My dearest Ruth, this is just a line to let you know dear that we are all safe, for which we are very thankful. We had a dreadful night again last night, it began about 8.45pm and we did not get to bed till 2.45am. It just sounded as though they were peppering away at our roof. Some of the tiles are broken on the other side of the road. I am afraid that they have done a lot of damage, we heard this morning they have got the Cathedral, but we don't know yet the extent of the damage. Some say they got Ford's Hospital, we do not know yet if that is right, but a bomb went right through Owen Owen stores to the ground floor and started a fire... In the raid on Saturday night two air raid wardens were killed by a delayed action bomb, it all happened in the road at the back of us, behind the church. Poor fellows, they had got everyone out of the houses and in a safe place and then for that to happen. We picked up a piece of shrapnel this morning, it is all over the place. I am sure you will be pleased to hear that I don't get a bit nervy or panicky; I just carry on with my knitting. It is no use making a fuss, it only makes it worse for others and we can't alter things.

The skies were no safer. Fighter pilot John Carpenter, now recovered after his spell in hospital, wrote home to his parents on 31 October to describe the narrow escape that he had experienced the day before.

More exciting events to report, yesterday morning while patrolling over Maidstone at 30,000 feet we ran into about eighty Me 109s, which turned to give fight. I dived down and had a good old burst at one of them, but before I had finished I was myself attacked by two 109s and I was absolutely peppered with cannon shells and machine gun fire. My instrument panel broke up in front of me for the fire came from over my shoulder. The engine started thumping and vibrating so much that I thought it might shake the wings off. But I found that by putting it into fine pitch the vibration was not so bad. Luckily the engine did not seize up for I managed to struggle back over the aerodrome.

This was the point I was dreading most for I had to come down through 3,000 feet of thick cloud without any instruments. This I managed to do with a bit of luck and I came out over the aerodrome. I put the undercarriage and flaps down and prayed that nothing would break before I was on the deck. I made an ordinary landing but at the end of the run one wheel slowly collapsed so that I was stuck in the middle of the aerodrome with one wheel up. When I got out and inspected the aeroplane, the flight sergeant counted over 300 holes in the fuselage, a piece of the propeller had been shot away, my wireless mast had been carried away by a cannon shell, in fact it looked something like a sieve. I was congratulated for bringing it back as it was and landing it without further damage on the aerodrome. I am claiming one 109 as a probable, which makes up a bit.

(Right) In this photograph by Cecil Beaton, the western bell towers of St Paul's Cathedral in London can be seen through an archway after the heavy incendiary raid of 29 December 1940.

In terms of the bombing, London continued to receive the greatest attention from the Luftwaffe during these final weeks of October, as recorded in George King's diary.

Thursday, 10 October. There was a lot of damage done last night, Son, including the smashing up of the High Altar in St Paul's, St Clement Danes Church, Covent Garden and Bush House. We are continually promised something to stop the night bombing, and I am beginning to think it will have to come quickly, or a good part of London will be in ruins. You will find many landmarks gone when you come home.

Tuesday, 22 October. Well, the bombardment of London from the air still goes on, and the people are standing it magnificently. Yesterday they were heartened by the news that Berlin had been heavily bombed, and that the French Channel ports are now a mass of ruins after the continuous hammering they have had. Our Mr Churchill broadcast in English and French last night, and it was a

Lower High Street in Southampton after the air raids of 30 November and 1 December 1940. During the six-hour raid, eight hundred high-explosive bombs were dropped. The water, gas and electricity supplies were cut off in many areas, and the local authorities were widely criticised as they struggled to cope with the aftermath of such intense bombing.

most powerful effort. Our time is coming, he said, and pointed out that we are slowly gaining control of the air. It gets a bit wearying, this regular nightly bombing and gunfire, but unfortunately we are all soldiers now and it is part of the price we have to pay for victory. I thank Heaven we do not live any closer to London.

Thursday, 31 October. The raids on London have decreased in intensity during the last few nights, and probably Hitler has realised there is nothing doing in that direction and he must turn elsewhere.

With bombing now the main German method for trying to break British resolve, and Fighter Command remaining a strong and effective deterrent against enemy air attacks, the immediate invasion threat had seemingly passed. The battle for air superiority was effectively over as far as the British were concerned, and 31 October was declared to be the official end date of the Battle of Britain. Yet neither side had won in any conventional sense. The final balance between Fighter Command and the Luftwaffe was not so different to how it had been at the beginning, although overall German losses had been much greater due to the vulnerability of their bomber aircraft; since 10 July, the RAF's Fighter Command had lost 915 aircraft and the Luftwaffe, some 1,733. Ultimately, the Battle of Britain therefore ended with a stalemate. The British were still isolated and in no position to launch an offensive into occupied Europe, yet neither could the Germans realistically consider invading and occupying Britain. The most important outcome was that British resolve had not been broken, and the country was as ready as ever to fight back.

*

The Germans, however, saw things in a somewhat different way and would continue with their ongoing campaign of forcing Britain to surrender. For them, the Battle of Britain and the bombing would carry on, running into the following year. Indeed, to the civilians on the receiving end of the regular air raids, as well as the RAF squadrons scrambled into action to deal with the aerial attackers, little had changed. Daylight attacks would continue alongside the more common night-time campaign, as described in the following account written by a Mrs Simpson, resident in Hornsey, north London. She describes an attack by a lone Heinkel 111 which had just attacked the nearby Crouch End marshalling yard in the early afternoon of Sunday, 3 November.

Most of the men were out tending their home-grown vegetables, etc. My father was asleep downstairs as he worked nights. My husband was having a bath, and I was gazing idly out of the window with my young baby by my side in her highchair. Suddenly this peaceful moment was disturbed by what sounded like 'pop-pop-pop', which incredibly turned out to be machine-gun fire from an

(Page 202) The heaviest raids on Manchester took place on consecutive nights from 22 to 24 December. The Free Trade Hall, Smithfield Market and St Anne's Church were destroyed, while Deansgate and Oxford Road were blocked with debris and unexploded bombs. More than 8,000 homes were destroyed or made uninhabitable.

(Page 203) Buildings burn in Manchester after a German air raid on the night of 23 December 1940.

Schoolgirls rest on part of a German bomber
which had crashed near their farmhouse, in a
photograph taken on 16 August 1940.

(Pages 204–205) Bomb damage in the centre
of Coventry after the devastating German air
raid during the night of 14 November 1940.

enemy aircraft; no sirens, no warnings of any kind as the plane came down so low over the house that the black crosses and other markings were clearly visible. I was absolutely mesmerised and couldn't move. The plane roared over the house twice, firing at the men in the gardens who rushed indoors and then rushed out again as soon as it had passed over, shaking their fists at the aircraft, and one can only imagine their language! I shall never forget their rage and frustration – it was like watching a film.

Meanwhile, my husband had joined me and we actually saw a stick of three bombs leave the plane and we were at last galvanised into action. We grabbed the baby, rushed downstairs and huddled together in the hall where we were joined by my father still in his nightshirt! With baby in the middle we clung together thinking every minute would be our last. The house shook and the front door blew open but we were still alive. In the moments that followed, my father said 'Where's your mother?' and minutes later she appeared through the back door, shaking from head to foot. She was a ghastly colour and looked as I imagined a ghost would look. She'd been bailing out the air raid shelter in the garden, and her first words were, 'How could you leave me all alone?' She had been through the First World War and the Zeppelin raids and was clearly in shock.

On its return flight home, the same German aircraft which had bothered Mrs Simpson attacked the nearby Feltham airfield with its machine guns from an altitude of 50 metres, followed by a barracks in Aldershot from only 30 metres. The Heinkel crew subsequently spotted a train and machine-gunned that. Clearly, the crew of this particular aircraft seized every opportunity to strike at their enemy; in their minds, the Battle of Britain was far from over.

The year 1940 ended with a number of particularly savage raids on British cities, with Liverpool and the rest of Merseyside suffering the worst bomb damage outside of London. On the night of 28/29 November Liverpool was hit by 350 tons of high-explosive bombs, and the city sustained further intense raids on consecutive nights just before Christmas. While the city's docks were the main target, the surrounding streets of terraced houses where dock workers and their families lived were also devastated.

Birmingham was Britain's third most-bombed city. It had suffered its first major raid in August 1940, but more followed in September and October. In a raid on 19/20 November, more than 400 tons of high-explosive bombs were dropped and one of the city's most important factories, the Birmingham Small Arms (BSA) works, was hit, killing 53 workers. Following their new tactic of hitting towns and cities consecutively in a deliberate attempt to prevent repairs being carried out, the Germans blitzed Birmingham again on the following two nights.

Some of the most significant bombing of the war was inflicted on the city of Coventry, an important engineering and armaments-producing centre, as recorded by George King in his diary. On the night of 14/15 November, German bombers had dropped 503 tons of high-explosive bombs and 30,000 incendiary bombs on the city.

> Sunday, 17 November. There is some bad news about Coventry, son. The Huns attacked the city last Thursday night, as they claim with 500 planes. 200 people were killed and 800 wounded; at least they are the published figures. Of course, the damage to property was tremendous, and even the fine old 14th century Cathedral is a mass of ruins. The King went down there at once, and I think it must have helped the people to see him. There is but one thought in this country, Son, the defeat of the beasts; but there is not quite enough burning hate for my liking. It makes me boil when I think of the awful sorrow and misery for which the Huns are responsible in this return to absolute barbarism.

The casualty figures were even higher than George King reported: some 568 people were killed and 850 seriously injured. Coventry Cathedral was famously destroyed, while almost a third of the city's housing was made uninhabitable and 35 per cent of its shops were ruined. In a relatively small city with a population of just over 200,000, everybody knew someone who had been killed or injured in the raid. A new verb, coventrieren ('to Coventrate'), was used by the Germans to describe this new level of destruction. The damage inflicted to the old medieval cathedral was particularly symbolic of the devastation being felt by the wider country and would become an iconic image of the Blitz.

Manchester too would suffer in the days immediately before Christmas in some particularly devastating raids. As another major industrial centre, Manchester was home to several heavy engineering works, including Metropolitan-Vickers and other munitions factories. These became key targets for the Luftwaffe, and on consecutive nights from 22 December until Christmas Eve, the city was attacked from the air. Almost 2,000 incendiary bombs were dropped, and a section of Manchester Piccadilly railway station was almost completely destroyed. Six hundred fires were started by incendiaries over two nights. Many of Manchester's 3,500 full- and part-time firefighters and Civil Defence workers had not returned from Liverpool, where they had been sent several days before to help fight fires caused by air raids on that city; this left the remaining fire services spread thinly across Manchester and the damage was therefore even worse than it would otherwise have been.

Then, on 29 December 1940, following some days of respite over the Christmas period, a terrible blow was inflicted on London, when in a single night German bombers dropped more than 100,000 bombs on the city. The extent of the fires which broke out around the docks and the East End led some to describe the night as 'the Second Great Fire of London'. Firefighters from the London Fire Brigade and others brought in from nearby counties tackled these blazes in exhausting and dangerous conditions. As George King recalled, the fires raged for days and ended up destroying a wider area of the city than the first 'Great Fire' of 1666.

> Tuesday, 31 December. Göring's swines celebrated my return to London by their most savage attack on London. They dropped thousands of incendiaries and large parts of the City have been burned. The Guildhall with its treasures has gone, together with many of Wren's beautiful churches. Pretty well all the buildings round St Paul's are burnt, but the Cathedral stands... Damn the swines!

In such a way, 1940 ended – the year in which the war had been brought to the very doorsteps of British people in a most immediate and terrible way. The Blitz, now increasingly distinct from the Battle of Britain once the invasion threat had dissipated, would continue into the New Year but peter out by May 1941. Such an intense campaign of aerial bombing would only start again on 21 January 1944 with a final 'Baby Blitz' that lasted for four months.

Chapter Eight

THE OUTCOME
OF THE BATTLE

Germany did not win the Battle of Britain. They failed to destroy Fighter Command or achieve air superiority over Britain, which were essential prerequisites to pave the way for an invasion. The sustained efforts of the Luftwaffe to bomb British cities into submission in 1940 had also proven unsuccessful. The Blitz would continue well into the following year, although the Luftwaffe's failure to attack key targets repeatedly and in an accurate and systematic way meant that they achieved few if any strategic victories. Whether the bombing was ultimately intended to destroy key industries or erode the morale of the civilian population, neither campaign worked as intended.

The true significance of the outcome of the Battle of Britain was not fully appreciated in an official capacity by the British until mid-November 1940 at the earliest, when Lord Dowding forwarded a report to the Air Ministry in which he made the following observation.

> the point to remember is that the losses sustained by the enemy were so great that heavy day attacks by bombers were brought to a standstill and that the Command did, in fact, win a notable victory; since, if the attacks had not been brought to a standstill, the invasion would have been facilitated and the war might well have been lost.

The success of the RAF, and Fighter Command in particular, in thwarting German attempts to wear down the nation until it had no option but to either surrender or submit to an enemy occupation was therefore recognised. But to many people in Britain towards the end of 1940, such a victory was far from obvious, since the outcome of the battle did not significantly reduce the scale of the threat still facing the country. This would not lessen until the Soviet Union and the United States finally joined the Allied cause later in the war.

The bombing campaign on British cities continued, and although people commonly believed by the end of 1940 that a German invasion had indeed been postponed by the result of the battle, they perceived it as only a temporary respite from the threat of occupation. The British government put a lot of effort into circulating advice in the form of pamphlets and propaganda in the spring of 1941 to prepare the population for a further invasion attempt, and new operational instructions were issued to the RAF in March about their role in attacking the invasion beaches. Indeed, the Luftwaffe was only one threat facing Britain in the second half of 1940, since the island nation was also struggling to survive against German efforts to isolate it by preventing imported goods and supplies arriving across the Atlantic. In addition, British and Commonwealth troops were committed to fighting a war against both Italians and Germans in North and East Africa, as well as the wider naval campaign in the Mediterranean.

Flying Officer Thomas Grier of No. 601 Squadron RAF stands on the wing of his Hurricane in Exeter, Devon, in November 1940.

(Pages 210–211) A newspaper seller in the street watches a 'dog fight' during the Battle of Britain and keeps score on his chalkboard. This image epitomises the idea of the 'Blitz spirit' in 1940.

From the German perspective, the Battle of Britain was far from over by November 1940 and would continue into spring 1941 through their ongoing efforts to bomb the nation into submission. The Luftwaffe's failure to destroy Britain's aerial defences had ruled out a quick win for Germany in the west, but there were other alternative strategies to pursue for the same ends. While their initial plan to destroy Fighter Command had failed, there was still the possibility of forcing the country to the point of exhaustion and thereby encouraging Britain to enter into peace negotiations. The aerial and naval blockade of ports might turn public opinion against the British leaders, or at the very least create better conditions for a future invasion and successful occupation. The Mediterranean campaign and the fighting in North Africa might also move in Hitler's favour, robbing Britain of valuable resources and fighting power. But whichever option the Germans pursued, lives would continue to be lost. Edith Heap served as a WAAF plotter in the operations room at RAF Debden in Essex, and had recently become engaged to marry Pilot Officer Denis Wissler, whom she served alongside.

The history bods have it that the battle ended on 31st October, but not to us – certainly the aerodromes were not being attacked so regularly, but the boys were always in the air it seemed. Then came 11th November, our squadrons were in the thick of it and just before we came off watch at 1200 hrs there was a cry of 'Blue 4 going down into the sea'. I was paralysed, luckily not frantically busy since Winifred and I were down on the floor, plotting on the blackboard, the only time we did. We did not know who it was, but I did – though I wasn't going to admit it. Denis still hadn't landed when I left the ops room. I didn't bother with lunch... I couldn't believe it and, of course, not being sure I allowed myself to hope. There was air/sea rescue etc. who had done sterling work. When I got back to Saffron, Bill was waiting for me and I told them where I had been. Yes, it was true, he was missing. No parachute.

That night I did not go on duty, due at midnight. Winifred had gone out with Jeff, and everyone else seemed to be elsewhere, so I went to bed but not to sleep, and lo and behold in the small hours my evening cook arrived with a cup of tea, saying she knew I wouldn't be asleep and sat down on the next bed and talked to me. I have never forgotten it and it was a great lesson to me. In the morning, I couldn't face the controller in his office, I'm such a water bucket, didn't want to break down, so Winifred did it for me with my request that there should be no telegram – I would go and tell his parents.

*

Despite not being an outright victory in the established sense of the term, the outcome of the Battle of Britain had been a positive one for Britain. But what were the key factors which determined the result?

A young boy places a Union Jack flag into the remains of his home, which was destroyed by an air raid on London in 1940.

(Pages 214–215) *Battle of Britain* by Paul Nash, 1941.

Soldiers pose with a Messerschmitt Bf 109E-4 which crash-landed at East Langdon in Kent on 24 August 1940. The pilot, Oberfeldwebel Beeck, was captured unhurt.

(Left) Prime Minister Winston Churchill inspects bomb damage inflicted to a hotel in Ramsgate, Kent, by Luftwaffe raids the night before, 28 August 1940.

Hurricane pilot Frederick Harrold was killed in action over Deal, Kent, on 28 September 1940 having been posted to No. 501 Squadron RAF only two days previously. This service dress uniform appears to have been worn by Harrold at the time of his death, as it displays evidence of battle damage under the left arm.

(Right) A selection of fragments recovered from Frederick Harrold's crashed Hurricane, excavated from the crash site in 1975.

(Below) Frederick Harrold's identity disc, likely to have been worn by him at the time of his death.

(Below right) Frederick Harrold's cigarette case, damaged during the crash which killed him.

In many ways the two opposing forces were evenly matched. Both had cutting-edge fighter aircraft, well-trained and brave pilots, and operational commanders of experience and distinction, and both sides showed a willingness to respond and adapt to the changing nature of the battle. Yet there existed a number of advantages and disadvantages which over time would influence the course of the battle in favour of Britain.

To begin with, the Germans were presented with a clear disadvantage in pursuing a campaign over enemy territory. This served to limit the range of their aircraft while reducing the effectiveness of their communications once airborne. While Fighter Command could call on further resources and backup when necessary, and had the added benefit of ground defence behind them in the manner of anti-aircraft guns, barrage balloons and searchlights, the German crews were out on a limb without support. Failure of one's aircraft, whether due to being hit in combat or simply running out of fuel, meant that the best-case scenario would likely be captivity as a prisoner of war. There were even dangers involving that circumstance, with local civilians being far from generous in their treatment of a newly captured enemy. There were certainly incidents of retribution against downed pilots, such as one example described by a clerk in the Royal Army Service Corps based near Tunbridge Wells in Kent who recalled a Luftwaffe pilot being brought in under an armed guard for interrogation.

> His plane had been shot down by one of the RN ships. After being interrogated, the NLO [Naval Liaison Officer] detailed me to escort him to the port and hand him over to the Royal Navy. The only transport available was a requisitioned open flat truck. Although he was handcuffed, he could not be accommodated alongside the driver, so had to sit on the floor of the truck with his back to the driver's cab, so it was suggested his guard would have to kneel in front of him with rifle and bayonet pointed close to his chest. This then presented another problem – the RASC are not issued with bayonets, though trained in their use. Eventually a bayonet was borrowed. The prisoner, who spoke very good English, was extremely belligerent and arrogant and throughout the twenty minutes rather bumpy journey subjected me constantly to a stream of invective, in English, about the decadent English and the certainty of Hitler winning the war. Before reaching the harbour the truck was halted by an angry crowd of local inhabitants demonstrating against the prisoner who was thought to have been responsible for bombing the local hospital. Some sought to climb on the truck and attack the prisoner.

The worst-case scenario, of course, was destruction in the air or a forced sea landing in the Channel, which would have meant almost certain death. From the British perspective alone, a crash in the Channel was likely to have fatal consequences, as Douglas Grice recalled. He had served as a pilot with No. 32 Squadron RAF.

> I was flying by myself a thousand or a couple of thousand feet higher than the rest of the squadron and slightly behind, weaving like mad, looking right, left, centre, up, down, mostly back. When suddenly I, out of the corner of my eye, saw a flash over my left wrist and the next moment of course the cockpit was full of flames. The heat was enormous and I'd done two things absolutely instinctively. My left hand had gone to the handle of the hood, my right hand had gone to the pin of my harness and I was pulling with both hands, and the next moment I was out in the open air. I'd made no attempt to jump out of that aircraft and of course I was straining back from the flames and the heat. And what I think had happened was, I was doing a left-hand turn and my aircraft had gone on turning over on its back and I'd just fallen out! Anyway, there I was falling away and I did actually remember my parachute drill, which was of course to wait before pulling the rip cord for two or three seconds. And I pulled it and there was a jerk and there I was floating down with a marvellous canopy and about a couple of miles inland. I could look down and see the land, so I thought, 'At least I won't be going into the sea.' Something seemed to have happened to my face – there were bits of skin flapping around my eyes! And my mouth felt very uncomfortable. Of course, I'd been burnt. Well, very shortly after that, I was over the coast and a few minutes later I was a mile out to sea, and a few minutes after that I was two miles out to sea. Well, the sea gradually approached and I wasn't a bit worried because I was coming down, going to splash down, only a couple of hundred yards from a little fishing trawler. Well, the splash happened and I got rid of my harness and looked round and there was the trawler and I waved like mad, and it eventually arrived and they hauled me on board.

Germany also suffered from a lack of aircraft and pilots to fly them. Despite the popular perception of Churchill's 'Few' defending their country against the might of the Luftwaffe, the number of single-engine fighter pilots available to Germany during the Battle of Britain remained below the equivalent figure for Fighter Command. At the beginning of September 1940, for instance, only 74 per cent of German fighter pilots were operationally ready; that month, their loss ratio amounted to just over 23 per cent.

It was also the case that the British aircraft industry outproduced that of Germany by quite a significant margin. This ensured that the RAF was supplied with a continuous flow of replacement aircraft to compensate for the higher loss rates experienced by Fighter Command. Their system of rotating squadrons and pilots also ensured that tiredness was kept to a minimum and each attack was met with sufficient force.

A further factor which contributed to the outcome of the battle could be seen as detrimental to both sides, although in the long run it served to benefit the British. Both Britain and Germany had to rely on somewhat poor and conflicting intelligence sources, which meant that neither power could accurately judge the true strength of the other. Since the outbreak of war, German intelligence had greatly underestimated the size of the RAF and the scale of the country's aircraft production. On 16 September 1940 they had calculated that the RAF had only 300 fighter aircraft left, including reserves, and a monthly output of 250. In reality, near that date Fighter Command could boast an operational strength of close to 656 aircraft, plus 202 in immediate reserve and 226 in preparation; their production output was around 428. Such misleading information generated a certain degree of complacency on the part of the German leadership when considering the likelihood of winning the Battle of Britain.

Conversely, the British Air Ministry's Air Intelligence Division had overestimated the size of Germany's air force and their aircraft production capacity. Despite holding the advantage of being able to decipher the secret German Enigma codes, intelligence officers misread the information they had obtained, misunderstanding statistics such as the balance between reserve and operational aircraft. The British therefore expected to fight a much stronger enemy, which perhaps goes some way towards explaining not only the British determination but also Churchill's references to 'The Few'. In relation to intelligence, it should also be pointed out that it was difficult for both sides to report losses accurately as far as aerial warfare was concerned. Claims of shooting down enemy aircraft were frequently exaggerated, not in a deliberate way but due to the ease with which 'victories' could be claimed by multiple pilots amid the outright confusion of intense combat.

We could also point to some strategic errors made by the Luftwaffe during the battle. Perhaps their most notable misjudgement was to shift the emphasis of their mission from attacking Fighter Command and their air bases to bombing the wider infrastructure sites. Again, inaccurate intelligence and resulting overconfidence go some way towards explaining this decision.

In terms of the RAF's strategic decisions, these were rather more positive and showed adaptability. By targeting enemy bombers above all else, the Spitfires and Hurricanes avoided being picked off by the bombers' fighter escorts as the Luftwaffe had intended. Instead, the German fighters discovered that they were required to protect their bomber fleet, thus severely limiting both their radius of action and manoeuvrability. The British also made full use of the new technology available to them. The early-warning value provided by Chain Home RDF and the Dowding System chain of command could not be underestimated and gave a crucial advantage to Fighter Command, ensuring that they were able to engage with the enemy as quickly as possible and in the most efficient way.

*

What was the human cost of the Battle of Britain? While the nature of wartime record-keeping means that it is difficult to present like-for-like comparisons, we know that Britain suffered 1,542 deaths among the ranks of RAF Fighter Command, Bomber Command and Coastal Command. This is against 2,585 killed from the Luftwaffe and 925 captured. The largest losses were among Bomber Command crews, which made up 718 of the total. Fighter Command suffered 544 deaths, which perhaps indicates the immense efficiency of what was already a fairly tiny force. No squadron escaped without comrades being killed, however, and the tangible fear of taking off in your aircraft for the very last time was widely experienced by all pilots. There was the mental cost too, with the intense experience of fighting the battle, both in the air as well as on the ground, having an acute effect on the mental health of so many of the participants. Harold Bird-Wilson, a pilot with No. 17 Squadron RAF, reflected on this many years later.

> You read many stories nowadays of pilots saying they weren't worried and weren't frightened when they saw little dots in the sky, which gradually increased in numbers and grew in size as they came from the French coast towards the English, over Kent and towards London. I maintain that if anybody says that they weren't frightened or apprehensive at such an occasion then I think he's a very bad liar, because you cannot help but get worried. I openly admit that I was worried and I was frightened at times. As the battle went on and on, we were praying for bad weather – it's the only time in England I think anybody ever prayed for bad weather. But somehow during the whole of the battle we had beautiful weather – sunshine and blue skies. And we prayed mighty hard. And fatigue broke into a chap's mentality in the most peculiar ways. Some really got the jitters and facial twitches and stuff like that. Others, as I did, I had nightmares at night. I admit it that I used to wake up in my dispersal hut, sleeping near – within 25 yards of – my aircraft and I was night-flying my Hurricane. This went on for quite a long time.

As well as the simple terror of having to face a relentless enemy in exceptionally dangerous circumstances, there were the feelings of blame experienced by those who had so far avoided death. Such survivor guilt was common, and even hospitalisation might be seen as an undeserved frustration for pilots eager to get back into the battle, like George Bennions.

> The first few weeks – I don't remember much about it, really. I was very concerned, very upset, feeling rather annoyed with myself for having been shot down so decisively and... I felt, I don't know, awful

The band of the RAF Regiment march past Buckingham Palace during the Battle of Britain Day parade, held in September 1943.

Battle of Britain Anniversary, 1943: RAF Parade at Buckingham Palace by Charles Cundall, 1943.

feeling really, terribly isolated. I couldn't see, I couldn't hear very well. I couldn't recognise people unless it was somebody very close to me. I felt so deflated, just as though half my life had been taken and the half wasn't worth bothering with. It was, I think, the worst period of my life.

My friend, the chap I'd joined up with from school, he was in ward three at East Grinstead. He'd been shot down flying a Hurricane. He was in ward three. He'd heard that I'd been admitted to the hospital. He'd sent a message along, could I go and see him? As I opened the door in ward three I saw what I can only describe now as the most horrifying thing that I have ever seen in my life. That was this chap, who had been badly burnt, really badly burnt. His hair was burnt off, his eyebrows were burnt off, his eyelids were burnt off – you could just see his staring eyes. His nose was burnt; there were just two holes in his face. His lips were badly burnt. And then when I looked down, his hands were burnt. I looked down at his feet also. His feet were burnt. I got through the door on crutches with a bit of a struggle. This chap started propelling a wheelchair down the ward. Halfway down he picked up a chair with his teeth. That's when I noticed how badly his lips were burnt. Then he brought this chair down the ward, threw it alongside me and said, 'Have a seat, old boy.' And I cried. I thought, 'What have I to complain about?' From then on everything fell into place.

*

The Battle of Britain – the HMSO publication from 1941 which heavily contributed towards the legend of the battle.

The lack of anything to signify a clear 'victory' in the traditional sense meant that it took a while before the Battle of Britain was represented in the way with which we are now familiar. When Churchill coined the term in June 1940, he was referring to the more general attempt by Germany to break British resolve, rather than specifically the air battle. Those who fought the battle itself would remain largely anonymous until years later. The fighter aces were not immediately glamorised, and their commanders were soon dispensed with after various behind-the-scenes machinations: Cyril Newall was replaced as chief of the air staff by Sir Charles Portal on 2 October 1940, while Lord Dowding was replaced as the head of Fighter Command by Sir William Sholto Douglas shortly before the end of the year.

It was not really until 1941, with the benefit of hindsight and once the Blitz was nearing its end, that people began to regard the Battle of Britain in the same way that it is generally perceived today: as a close-run struggle which would inspire future fighting. March 1941 saw publication by the Air Ministry of a 32-page pamphlet entitled *The Battle of Britain* which proved an immediate success, selling more than a million copies in Britain alone. Produced largely for propaganda purposes and also distributed within the United States and dominions, the pamphlet featured images of burning London which were accompanied by stirring, first-hand testimonies of the bombing. Perhaps this provided what the British people needed above all else: a reminder of the greater sense of purpose and unity. By bringing the war 'home', the Battle of Britain showed that everybody was involved in the conflict and could contribute in many different ways, even through making harsh sacrifices on a daily basis. By pulling its resources together, the country had successfully avoided enemy invasion. The war was now a People's War in every sense. The fighting spirit of a nation demoralised by the events in Europe over the last year had now been fully roused.

The Battle of Britain would receive the ultimate tribute of having a formal public anniversary granted to it; only the Battle of Trafalgar had previously been commemorated in this way. Just as the famous naval battle of 1805 was remembered as a decisive victory by the Royal Navy over the French and Spanish fleets, the Battle of Britain would mark a similarly important outcome against the German air force. Whether or not it was seen as an outright victory, the importance of the Battle of Britain lies in the fact that it marked the first time in the war that the violent fascist aggression of National Socialism was successfully confronted. It would take further years and many more sacrifices before the war was finally won, but in these terms the Battle of Britain served as the crucial first stage in turning the tide.

SOURCES

IWM Documents © IWM unless otherwise stated

Private papers of Major H-E Bob (Documents.788)

Private papers of D Bruce (Documents.4500)

Private papers of N Cameron (Documents.15134)

Private papers of Pilot Officer J M V Carpenter (Documents.2127)

Private papers of J W Clark (Documents.16049)

Private papers of H G Harris (Documents.4023) © Denise Cannon, daughter of H G Harris

Private papers of Lieutenant R W Holborow (Documents.15631) © Estate of R W Holborow

Private papers of G W King (Documents.3777)

Private papers of Mrs E M Kup (Documents.507)

Private papers of Mrs Ruth Oxer (Documents.20010)

Private papers of R Pountney (Documents.7937)

Private papers of Mrs L C Simpson (Documents.7952) © Donald Simpson, son of Mrs L C Simpson

Private papers of J L Sweetland (Documents.6546)

IWM Sound Archive © IWM unless otherwise stated

Roland Prosper Beaumont (10129)

George Bennions (10296)

Ronald Berry (11475)

Stanley Alan Clark (20304)

Jimmy Corbin (32057)

David George Samuel Richardson Cox (11510)

Hilda Majorie Cripps (18337)

Alan Deere (10478)

Wolfgang Julius Feodor Falck (11247)

Denys Gillam (10049)

James Alexander Goodson (11623)

Douglas Hamilton Grice (10897)

Rosemary Elizabeth Horstmann (10871)

Hugh Harold Allan Ironside (13101)

Samuel Valentine Love (6728)

Ludwik Alfred Martel (27233)

Ronald William Oates (17931)

Geoffrey Page (11103)

Mahinder Singh Pujji (18373)

Jeffrey Kindersley Quill (15456)

Cyril Sherwood (20398)

George Unwin (11544)

Joan Fleetwood Varley (28454)

Harold Bird-Wilson (10093)

Other

'The Airmen of the Battle of Britain', Battle of Britain London Monument, accessed March, 2022 <https://bbm.org.uk/the-airmen/>

Bickers, Richard Townshend, *The Battle of Britain* (New York: Salamander, 1990), appendix 24

Calder, Angus, *The People's War: Britain 1939–1945* (London: Jonathan Cape, 1969), p.145

Hillary, Richard, *The Last Enemy* (London: Macmillan, 1942), p.96

Hitler, Adolf, 'Adolf Hitler – Great speech to the German Reichstag', *der-fuehrer*, accessed February, 2022 <https://der-fuehrer.org/reden/english/40-07-19.htm>

Overy, Richard, *The Battle of Britain: Myth and Reality* (London: Penguin Books, 2010 edition), p. 32, p.50, p. 73, pp.114–7, p. 145, p.148

Report by Lord Dowding to the Air Ministry, 15 November 1940 (TNA, AIR 16/635), quoted in Overy, p.110

Winston, Churchill, 'The Few', International Churchill Society: Winston Churchill, accessed February, 2022 <https://winstonchurchill.org/resources/speeches/1940-the-finest-hour/the-few/> © Chartwell Trust. Reprinted by permission of Curtis Brown, London

Winston, Churchill, 'We Shall Fight on the Beaches', International Churchill Society: Winston Churchill, accessed February, 2022 <https://winstonchurchill.org/resources/speeches/1940-the-finest-hour/we-shall-fight-on-the-beaches/> © Chartwell Trust. Reprinted by permission of Curtis Brown, London

ACKNOWLEDGEMENTS

The author should like to thank the writers, families and copyright holders of those individuals whose personal testimony has been reproduced in this book. The Visual History series has allowed us to share some of the museum's best letters, diaries, memoirs and interviews with a wider audience, while also showcasing the huge variety of photographs, artwork and other objects from IWM's extensive collection. This book has been very much a team effort, and I would therefore also like to thank my colleagues from IWM's Publishing team (David Fenton, Madeleine James and Lara Bateman); designer Kirsty Macdiarmid; copy-editor Charlie Wilson; and curator Adrian Kerrison for his subject expertise.

IMAGE LIST

Introduction

Art.IWM ART LD 2123, Art.IWM PST 14972, O 2170, CH 1467, CH 1340, MH 26392

Chapter One

NYP 68075, Art.IWM PST 8490, HU 86082, HU 33149, HU 34702, HU 93720, N 228, HU 41241, A 17084, D 4847, H 2988, Art.IWM PST 4948 © The Royal Society for the Prevention of Accidents, H 4733, Art.IWM ART LD 644, Documents.11929/J, Documents.4972a, HU 104718

Chapter Two

HU 75542, MH 6041, HU 51040, HU 92609, HU 108206, MH 13382, HU 76020, CH 1367A, MH 6096, HU 4128, D 1417, CM 3513, CH 1414, Art.IWM ART LD 2321, CH 1534, CH 1436, HU 59071, CH 10629, CH 868, TR 2625, CH 1536, HU 54418, CH 1405, CH 1465

Chapter Three

Art.IWM ART LD 769, Art.IWM ART LD 626, H 2628, HU 69164, H 2628, HU 69164, HU 106341, HU 73424, HU 104481, HU 104490, HU 71114, Art.IWM PST 13837, H 2695, HU 72542, MH 24171

Chapter Four

CH 15331, CH 1451, D 12131, CH 737, HU 104482, Art.IWM ART LD 5735, CH 883, CH 1205, HU 93040, CH 15332, HU 67693, CH 15173, CH 1401, H 1291, HU 104540, CH 2477, HU 108212, MH 6547,

CH 7346, CH 1515, C45P60 © Sueddeutsche Zeitung Photo / Alamy Stock Photo, Documents.9357/A, CH 1471, MH 6115, D 12139, HU 24780, CH 7698

Chapter Five

CH 736, FX 68707, HU 54519A, CH 1550, CH 870, CH 1822, CH 1696, C 2418, HU 7960, GER 530, HU 104500, CH 1461, CH 1429

Chapter Six

Art.IWM ART 15672 3, IWM C 5424, HU 287, Art.IWM ART LD 1290, Art.IWM ART LD 485, H 4219, Art.IWM ART LD 838, MH 26395, Art.IWM ART 17977 © The Henry Moore Foundation, Art.IWM ART LD 1353, Art.IWM ART 15672 1, CH 1821, HU 104735

Chapter Seven

Art.IWM ART LD 866, UNI 9823, FEQ 418, EPH 2957, Documents.8948/A, Art.IWM ART 16537, Art.IWM ART LD 672, D 1576, D 1619, HU 104731, Documents.15134/A, HU 3376, CH 1823, CH 1829, H 5603, MH 2718, ZZZ 8205C, H 6319, H 6324, H 5600, HU 106837

Chapter Eight

HU 810, CH 1626, Art.IWM ART LD 1550, D 1303, H 3514, HU 67704, UNI 13724, EPH 10134, EQU 4486, EPH 10133, Art.IWM ART LD 2320, CH 11162, Art.IWM ART LD 3911, Documents.8948/B

INDEX

Grzeszczak, Flying Officer Bogdan *62–3*
gun crews 80
    see also anti-aircraft artillery

H

Halifax, Edward Wood, 1st Earl of *30*, 31, *33*, 42
Harris, Harry 110, 122
Harrold, Frederick 220, *220–1*
Heap, Edith 216
Heinkel He 111 *88–9*, *92–3*, *95*, 119, *119*, *140*, *144*, *172–3*, 193, *193–4*, 195, 201, 207
helmets 178, *178*
Henderson, Flight Officer Elspeth 137, *137*
Henneberg, Flying Officer Zdzisław *62–3*
Hess, Squadron Leader Alexander 'Sasha' *13*
Hewson, Miriam 195, 198
Hillary, Richard 146
Hitler, Adolf
    appeasement of 31
    attack, plan for 94
    invasion of Britain 36, 41–2, *46–7*, 50
    'Last Appeal to Reason' speech (19 July 1940) 42, *43*
    London, bombing of 158
Holborow, Richard 35
Hollyoak, Joyce *96–7*, 98
Home Guard *see* Local Defence Volunteers
horse-drawn artillery *24–5*
Horstmann, Rosemary 118
Hurricane *64–5*, *67*, *71*, *85–7*, 98, 101, *101*, 103, *136*, 148, *150*, 169, *213*, *221*

I

identity disc *221*
incendiary bombs 178
intelligence sources 226
    see also observation system
international pilots 49, *50*, 56, 58, *59*, 62, *62–5*, 70, *70*
invasion of Britain 36, 41–2, *41*, 175
Ironside, Hugh 84, 90
Italian air force *192*

J

Jodl, General Alfred *46–7*, 50
Jones, Flight Sergeant 66, 67
Junkers Ju 87 127, *127*, *142*
Junkers Ju 88 79, 125, *125*, 187, *188–9*

K

Keitel, Field Marshal Wilhelm *46–7*, 50
Kennington, Eric, *Sergeant M Eriksen of the Royal Norwegian Air Force Serving with the RAF 61*
Kent, Flight Lieutenant John A 'Kentowski' *62–3*
Kesselring, Field Marshal Albert 49, *49*
King, George 150–1, 154, 158, 174, 175, 200–1, 208, 209
Knight, Laura, *Corporal J D M Pearson GC, WAAF* 76, 77

L

Lancaster, Joan *96–7*, 98
Lane, Squadron Leader Brian 'Sandy' *149*
Leigh-Mallory, Air Vice-Marshal Trafford 69, *69*, 148
Liverpool 207
Local Defence Volunteers (Home Guard) 146
Łokuciewski, Pilot Officer Witold 'Tolo' *62–3*
London 158, 164, 169, 174, 178, 180, 184, 187, 200–1, 208–9, *217*
    Battle of Britain: The First Blitz (Gray) 168
    Buckingham Palace 174, *228–31*
    Finding an Unexploded Bomb... (Oppenheim) *182*
    A House Collapsing on Two Firemen... (Rosoman) *167*
    St Paul's Cathedral *152–3*, 154, 198, *199*
    Underground *156*, 158, *183*, 184, *185*
Love, Samuel 27
Luftwaffe
    advantages and disadvantages 222–3, 226–7
    air fleets 48
    aircraft 103, 105 *see also* Dornier; Heinkel; Junkers; Messerschmitt
    aircraft losses 171, 174, 175, 195, 201
    aircraft numbers 133, 223
    aircraft production 72–3
    bombing strategies 164, 169, 171, 178, 180
    commanders 48, 49, 56
    flying strategies 84, 90, 94, 132, 154, 226
    outcome of the Battle of Britain 212, 216
    pilots 27, 31, 48, *51*, *54*, 59, 222

M

Manchester 201, *202–3*, 208
Martel, Ludwik 56, 58
Merlin aircraft engines 99, *126*, 127